Endorsements

Mary Salamon has written the most practical guide for every citizen, let alone what every serious Christian needs, to understand how our Representational Democracy actually works. Every page clarifies in a direct way how each layer of our local, State and National government works and how individual citizens can understand this layered and complicated system. Many Christians think all levels of our government as confusing, corrupt, entangled in worldly values, dirty and beyond repair. They turn away from every mention of government while throwing their hands up in despair, feeling that average citizens could not possibly effect any change for the good. Christians know we are blessed with our form of government, but many are savoring the last days of the Republic and sadly believing there is no saving it now. In resignation, we are left to go on our lives just hoping nothing major will disrupt our freedoms and church community.

Mary shows us that there is another way to perceive our government! She shows us we can understand it and more importantly, steps laid out in this book will reduce our frustration and a sense of victimhood that characterize all too many Christians. Just as God is Lord over all of life, government is an area that important and Godly perspectives have much stability to add to it. Understanding there are steps that, beyond voting, every citizen can do to ensure our lives will be peaceful and actually benefit the weaker ones, protecting them and ordering our community lives.

Her section of study questions would be excellent to discuss at the family dinner table, in a small group or a prayer group. Specific questions help us to think logically and expand our knowledge. As they say, knowledge is power. Many voices have decried this decade where so much has careened out of control in society but very few answers have been proposed. This book lays a groundwork for needed knowledge, understanding and presents the original purpose of godly standards in government that have now been eroding away. Without criticizing current positions, she lays out a place to begin and a track to run on. I see this book as an answer to "What can I do?" that so many are asking now. We Christian citizens can do this! Take one thing and start.

Thanks, Mary, for this helpful and motivating book!

Virginia L. Chapman

Church Awakening Prayer Coordinator

*****

Mary Salamon's new book, *The Government and Its People— How The Church Can Participate in Government,* is a fresh and instructive primer in the basic role of the people of God as it pertains to society in general and the civil government in specific. The author skillfully weaves real life stories into this resourceful guide into the intimidating challenge of understanding the titles and duties of our civil leaders at every level. Mary also incorporates the mandate to pray for our leaders and does so in a very compelling manner I highly recommend this new and most timely teaching for citizens both young and old.

Barbara Ingmire

National Day of Prayer Task Force

National Area Leader West

RPN WA State Leader

THE GOVERNMENT
AND
ITS PEOPLE

HOW THE CHURCH CAN
PARTICIPATE IN GOVERNMENT

Mary Salamon

The Government and Its People
How the Church Can Participate In Government
by Mary Salamon

Cover by Amani Hansen
Editing by Allison Hitz and Jim Bryson
Layout by Jim Bryson

Dedication

The message of this book is dedicated to the Grace of God. I didn't pursue this message, the message pursued me. It eventually took me over and I was forced to write this book in order to get this message out of my heart and on paper. Government and Politics is not a popular subject, nor is it lighthearted to discuss and dissect. Even so, there are thousands of people that serve in government. This book is written to encourage and confirm that calling, but also to raise up thousands of Christians to answer the call to Civil Government. I want to thank my editors Allison Hitz and Jim Bryson. Alison began the journey with me and her work as an editor and proofreader are invaluable. Jim helped me finish the course with this project. Jim's experience as an editor brought me insight and helped me probe deeper into this subject as well as helping to add depth to my writing. The mountain of government needs to be climbed all the way to the top in order for the Gospel to continue to spread. This book is for all the climbers of that mountain.

Mary

Contents

Volume I

Why The Church Should
Participate In Government

Introduction to Volume I

For many years, I watched the news as a spectator. I cared little about state and world affairs. One reason was my upbringing. Our family was a sports family: football, baseball, softball, and basketball. Another reason was that my dad was a Teamsters Union employee and naturally gravitated to the Democratic Party. When asked what party affiliation we were, he'd boom out "Democrats!", adding that he hated Nixon. It was the same when Jehovah's Witnesses came to our door. "We're Catholics!" he'd say as he slammed the door. Ironically, we went to mass once a year. Yeah, you guessed it—Easter Sunday, adorned with all the fixings: a beautiful spring dress, an Easter bonnet, and white shiny shoes to complete the outfit.

Making matters worse, I continually heard this phrase in our home: "We never discuss politics and religion." As I grew into my adult years, I realized that it was a common saying with many people. And why not? It sounds so wise and philosophical. Yet today, I look at that phrase and think how ignorant and shallow it is. I know people who dodge these subjects to avoid combative discussions, but the downside is that at a certain level, there will always be parts of the relationship that will go unnoticed and unchallenged. As I look back on my upbringing, I realize that the reason my dad refused to discuss politics and religion is because we never participated in either culture.

In my early twenties, I became a Christian and joined a protestant church. I learned many wonderful things studying the Bible. Still, they believed that Christians were to separate themselves from the world and be fully engaged in church life instead. We were taught to engage people outside of the church only for the sake of evangelism. The core belief was that the more separated you were from the world, the more holy you were. Of course, we could engage in activities like sports or gardening, but even these activities could become idols if we spent more time weeding than reading our Bibles. Of course, politics and government were never discussed in this church. Instead, we heard:

"The church must obey God rather than men."

"We are not of this world. Our kingdom is a heavenly kingdom, *not* an earthly one."

And the final argument against engaging in politics, spoken with great conviction:

"Jesus was not political!"

Aside from my upbringing and current church environment, the fact was I never paid attention to politics and government due to my lack of understanding of how these worked. When I watched the news, I couldn't comprehend why particular issues and policies were geared a certain way. I felt the people running the government were exceptionally intelligent, as were the media people who reported it. Yet there were times when I would listen and say to myself, "Why can't I understand any of this?"

I remember watching Ronald Regan on the television say these famous words: "Mr. Gorbachev, tear down this wall!" At the time, it meant nothing to me. I was more concerned with my family, my faith, and myself. I believed that the worldly, earthly government was dark and that nothing good came out of it. I believed the most important governments that existed were the church government and family. I was taught that everything will be better when Jesus returns and that we were to occupy until he comes, keeping busy saving souls and doing religious activities.

Then something profound happened to me. I became a homeschooling mom.

Well, there was a bit more to it. To instruct my children, I was forced to look at certain subjects more closely. Through homeschooling conventions, workshops, and seminars, I learned about the importance of solid teaching on civics, government, and history. In my quest to give my sons the best education I could provide, I began to absorb books on our founding fathers and other national heroes. As I studied the curriculum to teach my children—easy-to-read books at first—I became obsessed with how amazing and blessed were our national leaders. I was stunned to learn that most were people of faith. I wept as I read about Abraham Lincoln, John Adams, and Daniel Webster. The crucial thing that resonated with me while studying was that God had placed his people in key, dominate, history-making roles. Those roles were *outside* the walls of the church and *inside* the very institutions I found to be oblique and religiously reprehensible.

Another profound influence—for me and millions of my generation—was the birth of talk radio.

Of course, conversation and family shows had been on the radio since the 1930s. However, this was the birth of *political* talk radio. The more I listened, the more I learned. I began to understand the issues, especially those important to my heart. I registered to vote and began keeping abreast of local, state, and national issues. I learned that politics is not hard to understand; a person just needs a good instructor. By listening to several radio hosts and the people calling in with their insights, opinions, and questions, I could comprehend complex political arguments that used to go right over my head.

Remarkably, changing my political views also changed my religious views. I realized that as a Christian—*especially* as a Christian—I had a responsibility to the country I called my home and in which I raised my children. According to Scripture, we are all given a *metron*—Greek for "a measure of rule." As citizens of the United States, our *metron* is the right to voice our opinion and give ourselves to different levels of government without fear of retribution.

Finally, the most profound revelation about government and my Christian faith was not that I had a rich heritage *nationally*, but that I had one *scripturally*. One day as I sat praying and mediating about the importance of Christians and government, the Lord showed me that almost every patriarch and prophet in Scripture either aided a government official or became one. It was like reading a *Who's Who of the Bible*. Government was established from the heart of God and given to His people. *"For the LORD is our judge, the LORD is our lawgiver, the LORD is our king; it is He who will save us"* (Isaiah 33:22). Any thinking person must conclude that even though Jesus is not political, he is the author of all righteous and just government, and His servants were governmental leaders.

Consider the following from Dr. Robert Putnam of Harvard University:

> *"Over the last two decades the number of office seekers in any year at all levels in the American body politic - from school board to town council - shrank by perhaps 15 percent. As a result of this decline, Americans lost*

more than a quarter million candidates annually to choose among. It is impossible to know what price we paid collectively for the loss of those potential grassroots leaders—not only in terms of talent and creativity, but also in terms of competitive pressure on incumbent officeholders."[1]

Dr. Robert Putnam

Peter and Isabel Malkin Professor of Public Policy

Harvard University

Imagine what our country would look like if Christians became the majority of the office holders in the United States. Scripture tells us that Christians embody the wisdom of God— wisdom that is pure, peaceable, gentle, full of mercy with good fruits, impartial and sincere (James 3:17). All these attributes given to Christians through Christ's wisdom are the exact attributes ALL government leaders desperately need to rule and judge.

I can only imagine what price our country has paid because of the ignorance taught in many churches that Christians should avoid politics and government. It is impossible to know but staggering to contemplate.

In fulfilling my quest, this book is ammunition for Christians. It comes fully loaded with the *why* and the *how* of governmental engagement.

Why should Christians participate in government?

It is our God-Given heritage.

How can Christians participate in government?

There are many creative and diverse ways to be involved in government from prayer to running for office.

This book examines the wonderful and awe-inspiring governmental roles that our forefathers were given and brings us to the present opportunities Christians can activate to make an impact on our country and the world.

Let's begin the journey and see where it takes us.

Mary Salamon

1

Worldviews

S hould Christians be involved in politics and government?
The answer depends on your worldview. In simple terms, a
worldview is how you see the world. James Sire's definition from
The Universe Next Door is this:

> A worldview is a commitment, a fundamental
> orientation of the heart, that can be expressed as a
> story or in a set of presuppositions (assumptions which
> may be true, partially true or entirely false) which we
> hold (consciously or subconsciously, consistently or
> inconsistently) about the basic constitution of reality,
> and that provides the foundation on which we live and
> move and have our being.[2]

A worldview reflects the fundamental orientation of a person's
heart. Christians, although united by a common God through
Jesus Christ our Savior, possess a wide range of worldviews that
affect how they see their role in government.

Consider the Scripture, *"Do not love the world or anything
in the world. If anyone loves the world, the love of the Father is not
in them"* (1 John 2:15). Depending on a person's heart orientation,
they could interpret this verse as justification for hating the
world—hate being the opposite of love. Another person with a
different worldview, however, would consider John 3:16: *"For God*

so loved the world that He gave His only begotten Son. That person would interpret 1 John 2:15 differently and so direct their heart to love the world in a way that seeks to improve it.

Interestingly, Christians with the worldview that loving the Father means hating the world are most likely to take the "watch and pray" approach to life, anticipating the imminent return of the Lord Jesus and therefore not being concerned with current events.

Other Christians see involvement in politics and government as futile based on the belief that God is in control of everything. They conclude that Christians are not mandated by God to change a world that God is already minutely controlling. The question arises, however: Is God in control of every level and form of government? If so, why do we still have evil dictators controlling countries, robbing and slaughtering their people, and wreaking havoc throughout the world? The unavoidable conclusion of a worldview based on a controlling God is that somehow the evil prevalent in our society is the judgment of God and therefore is from God himself.

The far-ranging opinions of Christian involvement in government also include the worldview that government is inherently evil and should be judged by the Lord. Consequently, people ask, "Why get involved in an institution that has no redeeming qualities?" After all, Thomas Paine wrote, "Government, even in its best state, is but a necessary evil; in its worst state an intolerable one."[3]

Gregory Boyd, in *God of the Possible*, presents a cogent argument for the opposite viewpoint:

> When we rid ourselves of any lingering suspicion that
> evil somehow fits into the eternal purposes of God,
> we are more inclined to do something about it. Jesus

spent his entire ministry revolting against the evil he confronted. He never suggested that any of the physical or spiritual afflictions he confronted somehow fit into his Father's plan. Rather, he confronted these things as coming from the Devil and carried out the Father's plan by healing people and delivering them. We who are Christ's disciples should follow our Master's lead.[4]

There could be several reasons why a person believes that government is evil and cannot be trusted. The first and strongest reason is that of injustice. When a person suffers unjustly from the government and no one comes to their aide, it causes deep mistrust and bitterness that can permeate many generations.

Others would counter, however, that while government has not always been fair and pure, we must recognize that this is due to the people in government positions and not government itself. When those holding authority rule unjustly through greed and lust for power, they cause great harm to others trying to live a peaceable life.

• So, does God want Christians involved in politics and government, shaping the world according to his will? Or does he expect believers to shun the political system and, as some would believe, *"Come out from among them and be separate,"* (2 Corinthians 6:17 NKJV).

We need to consider the nature of government before making up our minds on the issue. What do we mean, exactly, by "government"?

From a Biblical perspective, government exists to protect the people. This is why, when government fails in that purpose, it causes fear and anger in the hearts of people. Government is a creation from the heart of God, and as such is rooted in God's will.

He established government at the beginning of creation when he created humankind to rule.

> *So God created man in His own image; in the image of God He created him; male and female He created them. Then God blessed them, and God said to them, "Be fruitful and multiply; fill the earth and subdue it; have dominion over the fish of the sea, over the birds of the air, and over every living thing that moves on the earth."*
>
> Genesis 1:27-28

Notice the phrase *"have dominion over...."* Obviously, dominion is equated with ruling and governing. And unless one assumes that man's rule included the abuse of everything under his authority—this was pre-fall, after all—it stands to reason that this God-given authoritarian structure was benevolent.

Interestingly, the first governing institution created by God was marriage. It even preceded the commissioning of Genesis 1:28. We know this by the account given in Genesis 1:27 above. Note that God's commission was to *"them,"* as in *"male and female He created them...."* As in *two*, joined as *one*. In a word: marriage.

Elsewhere in Scripture, the Bible further delineates this governmental relationship, saying that the husband is the head of the wife.

> *For the husband is the head of the wife as Christ is the head of the church, his body, of which he is the Savior.*
>
> Ephesians 5:32

Clearly, the husband has been given authority over the wife. But why? The chief reason is to protect her, as understood by the phrase *"as Christ is the head of the church."* Jesus first and foremost protects his church out of love and from the strength that comes from ruling through God.

Using marital government as an example, when a husband fails to protect his wife, or in some cases controls and abuses her, he causes the institution of marriage to be distrusted. However, it is not that marital government is inherently evil, only that some people within marriage are evil. The institution itself is from God and is good.

Consider the role of government in property ownership. In most forms of government, there are laws and rules (procedures) in place to protect a person's right to own property. When someone tries to steal a person's property, the government's function is to declare such actions illegal and take appropriate steps to thwart the theft, thereby protecting the owner. Without such protections, ownership of anything would require constant warfare.

Of course, history tells us of unlawful confiscations of property by governments acting with impunity, of blatant racism and abuse of opposition. These glaring injustices are difficult to ignore and are often the reason that some embrace the worldview of *"come out and be separate."* By obeying a single Scripture—one that agrees with their worldview—they feel justified in ignoring the many other Scriptures that promote involvement in government, as well as denigrating opposing worldviews as "worldly."

However, the same abuses that cause some Christians to retreat drive other Christians to the worldview that not only should they be involved in government, but that they are *vital* to establishing God's principles and order at every level of government throughout the world. This perspective draws from Scriptures such as Jesus' parable of the ten talents.

The Government and Its People

And he called his ten servants, and delivered them
ten pounds, and said unto them, "Occupy till I come."

Luke 19:13 KJV

While this parable has far-reaching implications, at the very least, it should counteract the worldview based solely on *"come out and be separate."* The definition of "occupy" used in Jesus' phrase, *"occupy till I come,"* is this:

> *To take or fill up space; to be a resident or tenant; to hold a position or office; to take possession and control of a place, as by military invasion.*[5]

It is difficult to derive justification from this Scripture for being passive or complacent. A person who is occupying is active, aggressive, and engaged with the people, places, and events that surround him or her.

In looking to the Bible as God's word—the expression of his authority and will—we observe that the writers of the New Testament often refer to the patriarchs' and the prophets' lives as examples of how we should conduct our lives. Peering into their experiences gives us insight to the way God leads a righteous person's life. We can learn from their mistakes and victories, their authority and power, how they were appointed and positioned by God. Like gazing into a precious jewel with diverse facets, so it is when studying the people of the Bible. It holds layers of information, knowledge, wisdom, and understanding.

Many biblical leaders were involved in government. In fact, most of the patriarchs and prophets were either governmental leaders themselves, or they influenced top leaders and officials of their day. Consider how Jesus referred to Christians:

"You are the salt of the earth. But if the salt loses its saltiness, how can it be made salty again? It is no longer good for anything, except to be thrown out and trampled underfoot. You are the light of the world. A town built on a hill cannot be hidden.

Matthew 5:13-14

Light and salt are more than poetic symbols that we meditate on in our devotions. We must consider what actions coincide with being the light in the world and the salt of the earth. Light pierces, consumes, and fills the darkness. Salt was used as a preservative in the ancient world to ward off corruption. Jesus said that Christians are the salt of the earth. Throughout the Bible, salt was used for blessing to establish covenant and issuing judgment. If Christians are salt, we can inhibit the corruption of sin in this world with the living gospel.

Throughout our study, we will examine evidence supporting the belief that the Christian community should be actively involved in the political process and hold governmental offices at every level: neighborhood, city, county, state, and country. The Christian community is under a clarion call of God to fill the darkness with light and ward off corruption, not only the political world but the entire world and everything in it.

2

Where Government Begins

I live in Washington state, a place where many pride themselves on being self-sufficient. We are the state of Lewis and Clark, those intrepid explorers who forged the way to the Pacific Northwest in a bold, rugged fashion. (Led by a very pregnant Native American squaw, incidentally.) Indeed, my nation, the United States, is known for the independent attitudes of its populace. We are citizens who believe in pulling ourselves up by our bootstraps. And yet, we are interconnected, dependent on each other in ways we do not always appreciate. Some of that connectivity is in the form of laws.

Whether we acknowledge them or not, rules and authority govern our everyday lives. Everywhere a person goes, authority rules over them. When we get into our cars, we better have up-to-date registration and insurance. As we drive away, must obey traffic laws. At work, our employer has authority over us. Rules and the authority they convey are everywhere—restaurants, grocery stores, schools, even in our homes. We even need a building permit to add a room to our house—our very own house! Everything has an associated rule to follow.

Why?

For the sake of order, peace, and safety.

So, where does authority come from? God, of course. It is not man-made; it was established from the beginning.

> *For by him all things were created, in heaven and on earth, visible and invisible, whether thrones or dominions or rulers or authorities—all things were created through him and for him.*
>
> Colossians 1:16 (ESV)

God created a world that runs on authority, and he instituted government to administer that authority, bringing peace and order to our lives.

Let's look closer at the tiers of authority that God created as identified in Colossians.

Throne

- a ceremonial seat for rulers
- a chair of state having a footstool
- assigned to kings and queens, hence, royal power
- representing God's throne as the governor of the world
- representing Jesus Christ, the King of Kings, partner and assistant in the divine administration, hence all divine power belongs to Christ

Dominion

- power, lordship

Principalities:

- beginning, origin
- the person or thing that commences, the first person or thing in a series, the leader
- that by which anything begins to be, the active cause
- the extremity
- the first place of ruling angels and demons

Power

- choice
- liberty to do as one pleases
- leave or permission
- physical or mental power
- the ability or strength one possesses or exercises.
- authority (influence) and of right (privilege)
- rule or government (the power of him whose will and commands must be submitted to by others and obeyed)

  a. universally: authority over all mankind.

  b. specifically: the power of judicial decisions; the authority to manage domestic affairs

  c. metonymically: a thing subject to authority or rule; jurisdiction; one who possess authority; a ruler, a human magistrate.[6]

This covers every level of power, government, and authority in this world and beyond. Nothing and no one is outside God's authority, and Scripture says that all of this has all been given to Jesus.

> *All authority [all power of rule] in heaven and on earth has been given to me.*
>
> Matthew 28:18 (AMP)

Other scriptures continue this idea.

> *Who is gone into heaven and is on the right hand of God; angels and authorities and powers being made subject unto him.*
>
> 1 Peter 3:22 (ESV)

> *Far above all rule and authority and power and dominion, and above every name that is named, not only in this age but also in the one to come.*
>
> Ephesians 1:21 (ESV)

And ye are complete in him, which is the head of all principality and power

Colossians 2:10 (KJV).

For to us a child is born, a son is given; and the government will be upon his shoulder, and his name will be called Wonderful Counselor, Mighty God, Everlasting Father, Prince of Peace. Of the increase of his government and of peace there will be no end, upon the throne of David, and over his kingdom to establish it and uphold it with justice and with righteousness from this time forth and forever more.

Isaiah 9:6-7 (ESV)

Notice from Isaiah that God's government never ends. It continues to grow and expand. We will never escape it, nor should we.

So if God instituted governing and government, when did this government begin? For us, it began *"In the beginning,"* when God created the heavens and the earth, as recorded in the book of Genesis. It expanded with the creation of man and his governance.

So, God created man in his own image, in the image of God he created him; male and female he created them. And God blessed them. And God said to them, "Be fruitful and multiply and fill the earth and subdue it, and have dominion over the fish of the sea and over the birds of the heavens and over every living thing that moves on the earth."

Genesis 1:27- 28(ESV)

According to Pat Robertson in his book, *The Secret Kingdom:* Almighty God wants us to recapture the dominion man held in the beginning… The Genesis account uses two colorful words to describe this. One, *radah,* we translate 'dominion.' Man was to have dominion. The word means to 'rule over' or 'tread down,' as with grapes. It comes from a Hebrew root meaning 'spread out' or 'prostrate.' The picture we get from it is one of all the creation spread out before man, whose dominion would extend wherever his feet trod.

The other word, *kabash*, is translated 'subdue.' Man was told to subdue the earth. The root means 'to trample underfoot,' as one would do when washing dirty clothes. Therefore, in *kabash* we have in part the concept of separating good from evil by force. With the first word, *radah*, God gives man the authority to govern all that is willing to be governed. With the second, *kabash*, He grants man authority over the untamed and the rebellious. In both instances, God gave man a sweeping and total mandate of dominion over this planet and everything in it."[7]

In other words, God, who is supreme and has all authority, transferred that authority to humankind to rule and govern by the order He set in motion when He created the earth. While this may sound good at first, it presents an enormous challenge, one that humankind was never intended to face alone.

How do we carry out our God-given dominion and authority? Clearly, we do it through the institution of government. This is how we separate good and evil, the wise and the foolish, the just and the unjust. With the wisdom and mercy of God, we use laws, ordinances, and rules to live, govern, and reign in this world. This is what God had in mind when He commissioned Adam and Eve.

Throughout the Bible, we see God delegating, transferring, and imparting His authority to people he has chosen to fulfill His plan for humankind. The forerunners, patriarchs, and prophets had specific roles to fill, and today, the Church has specific roles to fill. One role is to engage in modern government. In the proceeding chapters, we will examine how God appointed, prepared, and anointed his servants in governmental positions, establishing His will upon the earth and setting the example for us to follow.

3

<u>Process</u>

As we study the lives of the servants of God who were chosen to be in governmental roles, a dominate element stands out: process. This is the process which these chosen people endured to fulfill their role in God's plan. It was a process of qualification consisting of training, testing, even sorting. Not everyone made it, but those who did served God mightily.

When we peer into the lives of forerunners like Joseph, Moses, and David, we discover that their processes were similar. Yes, they were naturally prepared to rule, but they were also tested and tried every way imaginable, their human spirits stretched, their hearts broken, their wills brought into conformity with God's will. There was nothing easy about these processes, and we are naïve to expect anything different today.

Process

By definition, the word "process" means, "continuous series of actions meant to accomplish some result." The Lord God created process. As such, He is in the midst of the process. Why people endure tests and trials can only be understood when evaluating God's purposes for a process. In our study, we can view this two ways:

1. the micro-process (detailed)
2. the macro-process (big picture)

The micro-process consists of the daily details of trials and testing, revealing how we respond to our unique circumstances. Through daily perseverance, we see the issues of our heart—our thoughts, motives, passions, and character traits comprising our personality. We evaluate our decision making; we face our mistakes and the needs they highlight. We discover how God uses the tiniest detail to enlarge our heart, to correct a deformity, and to perfect our soul.

Through the macro-process, we see how the Lord God takes things away while adding other things. The measuring scales are in His hands. While the micro-process is fascinating to study, it's the macro-process that reveals how the minute details fit together to form a larger picture. It's like a recipe. If want a perfect loaf of bread, the ingredients must be put together exactly as the recipe dictates. In these endeavors, we learn that there is a balance to perfection: not too much salt, just enough flour, warm water for yeast (not hot), and exact rising times. The final product—the bread—only comes out perfectly when we understand the importance of everything that goes into it. We can't take details for granted; a perfect loaf doesn't happen automatically. It takes time and effort. Nothing appears out of nowhere; even God's Spirt hovered over the faceless deep before God spoke creation into existence. And so it is for God's plan for His chosen servants. In His process, we learn to be patient and intentional.

Everything we know in our lives has an associated process. The macro-process reveals life as a whole—the big picture. To deny process in our lives is to deny our existence. Humankind is created for a God-given purpose and we are progressing to fill that purpose. Each generation is handed the torch from the previous generation to continue to walk out God's original mandate to be fruitful, multiply, and have dominion while living on this earth. Throughout history, we see how God is intricately moving humankind—how He intervenes, gets involved, blesses with innovation and invention, and increases knowledge and wisdom to human beings. We don't always see the hand of God at the micro-level, but it's hard to miss at the macro-level. The macro-level displays the positioning and timing of our God and reveals His grand purposes.

> *To the intent that the living may know that the Most High [God] rules the kingdom of mankind and gives it to whomever He will and sets over it the humblest and lowliest of men.*
>
> Daniel 4:17 (AMP)

The men and women of God recorded in the Bible were humble and lowly, though not at first, but they became that way by the shaping hand of God as He prepared them to rule and reign, thus establishing His will for humanity.

> *His intent was that now, through the church, the manifold wisdom of God should be made known to the rulers and authorities in the heavenly realms...*
>
> Ephesians 3:10

The Government and Its People

4

Joseph

Contrary to our Western worldview, the Bible identifies its leaders not as rugged individuals but as contributors to their family lineage, both natural and spiritual. As such, the God-given purpose of the patriarch Joseph's life did not begin with Joseph. It began with Jacob and Rachel, his parents. Jacob loved Rachel and wanted to marry her, but he had to marry her sister Leah first. So, he labored under their father for fourteen more years to finally have Rachel. After they married, several years passed before Rachel was able to conceive. Both she and Jacob went through dark trials and deep processes to have Joseph. Rachel was tried and tested time after time, watching her sister Leah give birth to one son after another for Jacob. Rachel lived in anguish and humiliation, and at one point she even wanted to die because of her infertility. When her son Joseph was finally born, she cried out, *"God has taken away my reproach"* (Genesis 30:23). Rachel was humbled from the beginning of her relationship with Jacob, not knowing she would birth a world leader leading to the Savior of the world. It was the process that qualified her.

Through this process, Jacob had twelve sons, including Joseph and Benjamin from Rachel. The Bible says that Jacob favored

Joseph and kept him close. He even presented Joseph with a robe of many colors. Jacob loved his son Joseph more than all the others and likely doted on him. Because of Jacob's favoritism, however, sibling rivalry and jealousy arose between Joseph and his brothers.

> *But when his brothers saw that their father loved him more than all his brothers, they hated him and could not speak peacefully to him.*
>
> Genesis 37:4 (ESV)

This was probably made worse by a sense of entitlement on Joseph's part. (Read: spoiled.) Scripture doesn't specify this, but any parent will recognize the dynamic. For example, we read of Joseph running to his father and giving a bad report about his brothers' activities. Let's face it: the kid was a tattle-tale.

Unfortunately, Joseph then instills more hatred and jealousy by sharing a dream he had from God. In one dream, he declares:

> *He said to them, "Hear this dream that I have dreamed: Behold, we were binding sheaves in the field, and behold, my sheaf arose and stood upright. And behold, your sheaves gathered around it and bowed down to my sheaf." His brothers said to him, "Are you indeed to reign over us? Or are you indeed to rule over us?" So they hated him even more for his dreams and for his words.*
>
> Genesis 37:6-8 (ESV)

Not content to leave well enough alone, Joseph shares another dream with his family, and the results are predictable.

> *Then he dreamed another dream and told it to his brothers and said, "Behold, I have dreamed another dream. Behold, the sun, the moon, and eleven stars were bowing down to me." But when he told it to his*

*father and to his brothers, his father rebuked him
and said to him, "What is this dream that you have
dreamed? Shall I and your mother and your brothers
indeed come to bow ourselves to the ground before
you?" And his brothers were jealous of him, but his
father kept the saying in mind.*

Genesis 37:9-11 (ESV)

You have to wonder if this kid was naïve or simply possessed of
a death-wish. Either way, he sure didn't help his standing with his
brothers. But remarkably, his actions ultimately placed him exactly
where God wanted him.

Thus began the process of Joseph's journey in preparation for
his life's call and destiny, even as he was dealt one injustice after
another. He was sold into slavery to the Egyptians by his brothers.
He became a slave in a man's household named Potiphar.

According to Dr. Charles Aling, Joseph would have been an
Asiatic slave in the middle kingdom of Egypt. "One of the most
common titles held by male Asiatic slaves was that of 'household
servant.'" These slaves did a variety of tasks: serving, cooking,
cleaning, and waiting on the master and his wife and children.
Joseph was faithful and favored, so according to Scripture Potiphar
made him steward over his entire household.[8]

Charles Aling continues:

Two of his subsidiary titles were "Scribe of Offerings"
and "Chief of Agricultural slaves." The first proves that
he was literate, and the second shows us his primary
duty, the supervision of his master's agricultural
estates. . . . This indicates two things about Joseph.
First, he was literate. He would have to be to hold a
stewardship. How and when he learned to read and

write the complex Egyptian language is not known. Perhaps it was when he was a household servant of Potiphar. In any case, we may assume that Joseph was a quick and diligent student. Secondly, as a steward, Joseph would have been in charge of the agricultural holdings of his master, Potiphar. We should remember that ancient Egypt did not have a money economy as we know it today, and officials such as Potiphar would have been paid for their work by being allowed the use or ownership of farmlands. Potiphar would not have the time or perhaps even the skills to supervise the land and its cultivation himself; hence the necessity for a steward. We remember too that Joseph came from an agricultural family, and presumably already had extensive knowledge of farming techniques and farm animals.[9]

This was the beginning of an extensive preparation for Joseph to fill his future governmental role. (Spoiler alert: He becomes prime minister of Egypt, second only to Pharaoh.) To run Potiphar's household, Joseph had to learn to read and write the Egyptian language. It makes perfect sense, doesn't it? A person would have to know the language thoroughly to rule its nation. So, being taken into Egypt was not a punishment from God but instead a thorough preparation. It took time to prepare Joseph. His training included learning the language, being immersed in the culture, and understanding the economy. The Scriptures state that Potiphar's entire household was blessed because of Joseph.

Things went well for Joseph until another injustice happened to him. Joseph was wrongly accused of assault by Potiphar's wife. He soon found himself in prison. According to Charles Aling:

Joseph

As the Genesis account states, there was a "Warden" or "Overseer of the Prison," who was assisted by a large staff of clerks and scribes. Record keeping at such an institution was as important to the ancient Egyptians as it is in a modern prison. The actual title Overseer of the Prison is not commonly found in Egyptian inscriptions, but examples do exist from the Middle Kingdom, the time of Joseph.

One of the chief assistants to the Warden or Overseer was the "Scribe of the Prison." In Genesis 39:22 we are told that Joseph was promoted to high office in the prison. Since Joseph was literate, as we have seen from the fact that he served as steward in the household of Potiphar, it seems probable that he was promoted to Scribe of the Prison. As such, he would not only have been the right-hand man of the Warden, but he also would have been in charge of all the records of the institution.[10]

Yes, Joseph was favored once again. According to Genesis:

The Lord was with Joseph and showed him steadfast love and gave him favor in the sight of the keeper of the prison. And the keeper of the prison put Joseph in charge of all the prisoners who were in the prison. Whatever was done there, he was the one who did it. The keeper of the prison paid no attention to anything that was in Joseph's charge, because the Lord was with him. And whatever he did, the Lord made it succeed.

Genesis 39:21-23 (ESV)

Being the right-hand man of the warden meant that Joseph had full access to everyone entering and leaving the prison. Meanwhile, he was given the gift of dreams and their interpretation. Remarkably, when Pharaoh's butler and baker were sent to prison, they both had dreams. Joseph was able to interpret their dreams, and when the butler was released, Joseph asked the butler to remember him. According to Charles Aling, the butler was actually a cupbearer to Pharaoh.[11] He would have been in attendance serving Pharaoh all his beverages and so be in position to have Pharaoh's ear. He would have been the perfect man to plead Joseph's case, but the cupbearer forgot Joseph. Then came the day that the king had a dream that he could not interpret. The cupbearer finally told the king about Joseph's gift of interpreting dreams.

In Genesis 41, Pharaoh had two dreams. In one dream he was standing by the Nile,

> *And behold, there came up out of the Nile seven cows attractive and plump, and they fed in the reed grass. And behold, seven other cows, ugly and thin, came up out of the Nile after them, and stood by the other cows on the bank of the Nile. And the ugly, thin cows ate up the seven attractive, plump cows.*
>
> Genesis 41:2-4 (ESV)

Then Pharaoh had a second dream.

> *And behold, seven ears of grain, plump and good, were growing on one stalk. And behold, after them sprouted seven ears, thin and blighted by the east wind. And the thin ears swallowed up the seven plump, full ears.*
>
> Genesis 41:5-7

Joseph finally appeared before Pharaoh, and he was able to interpret the dreams. He explained to Pharaoh about a future famine coming to Egypt. Joseph was then given instruction from

God on how to prepare for the coming famine. He did such a good job protecting Egypt from starvation that God gave him favor with Pharaoh. Joseph was exalted to the second in command in all of Egypt—the most powerful country in the Middle East. Joseph ultimately became a father to Pharaoh, the lord of Pharaoh's entire household, and ruler of all Egypt under Pharaoh (Genesis 45:8 ESV).

According to Charles Aling:

> The main job of the Chief Steward was the detailed supervision of the King's personal agricultural estates, the number of which would have been vast. This fits well with Joseph's advice regarding the coming years of plenty and the following years of famine. As Chief Steward, Joseph would be well placed to prepare for the coming famine during the years of more abundant production.
>
> It is interesting to observe that another specific responsibility of the Chief Steward was to take charge of the royal granaries, where the agricultural wealth of the nation was stored. As the person in charge of these great storehouses, Joseph was ideally placed for carrying out his suggestion to store food during the good years for the bad.[12]

Another title given to Joseph was "Ruler of all Egypt." This, according to Aling, could very well have been the position of Vizier of Egypt. This is strongly supported, and, if he was Vizier, Joseph's duties would have been similar to what we know as an ambassador and high official. Aling describes it as follows:

> There are Egyptian inscriptions that describe the duties of the Vizier of Egypt.... Several texts exist

which describe in great detail the duties and powers of the office of Vizier.

The Vizier was the chief record keeper of the government records, was the supervisor of the government in general, appointed lower officials of government to office, controlled access to the person of the Pharaoh, and generally supervised construction work and industry in Egypt's state-run economy. More pertinent to Joseph, the Vizier also was in charge of agricultural production, just what he needed to care for God's people in the time of famine.

Also, another power held by the Vizier has great interest in regard to the Joseph story. Only the Vizier welcomed foreign embassies coming into Egypt. So, when Joseph's brothers came to Egypt for food, they would normally meet with the Vizier. And, Joseph was the man they met.[13]

The account in the Bible demonstrates that God's calling and destiny for Joseph was to a position in one of the highest levels of Egyptian government—a position in a worldly government where the Lord gave him influence and power along with great authority to fulfill God's plan. Joseph's suffering, pruning, and testing were a preparation to fulfill a world-changing position in government.

What positions in our government today can we compare to those Joseph held so long ago? Joseph was a world leader, and he was used to save a nation. In our present day, the positions filled can be interpreted in several ways. There are problems in our environment that need answers. Who will be the ones to solve our nation's energy crisis? Who will be the ones to aid third-world nations in their fight against poverty and hunger? God is not just choosing one Joseph; Joseph is just an example for us to observe. God is looking for thousands of Josephs to save the world.

Are you one of them?

5

Moses

Of all the patriarchs in the Bible, Moses stands as one of the greatest men who ever lived. If we believe the Bible is the inspired Word of God, then we must acknowledge that Moses was an amazing human being. No one else acted in the various offices and capacities as he did. He was a deliverer, a military hero, a prophet, a judge, and a lawgiver. He established a new religious system and integrated civil laws with religious observances. He wrote the first five books of the Bible, including the history and law of God's people. Finally, he brought the people out of their bondage in Egypt, led them through a dark wilderness season, and brought them to the brink of entering the Promised Land, passing the reins of leadership to his groomed successor Joshua.

Yet, it didn't start that way. In fact, it was many long years and much travail until Moses was prepared for the role God had for him. Let's look closer into Moses' preparation for his role in active government.

The process through which Moses became an outstanding leader was filled with suffering, trials, and intense training, coupled with faith, perseverance, signs, wonders, and miracles. Just as in the case of Joseph's parents who endured testing and trials, so it was with Moses's parents. Moses was born in Egypt at a time where the Bible says:

> There arose a new king over Egypt, who did not know Joseph. And he said to his people, "Behold, the people of Israel are too many and too mighty for us. Come, let us deal shrewdly with them, lest they multiply, and, if war breaks out, they join our enemies and fight against us and escape from the land." Therefore they set taskmasters over them to afflict them with heavy burdens.... But the more they were oppressed, the more they multiplied and the more they spread abroad. And the Egyptians were in dread of the people of Israel.... In all their work they ruthlessly made them work as slaves.

> Exodus 1:8-14 (ESV)

Despite Pharaoh's ardent desires, however, the people of Israel continued to multiply. Eventually, Pharaoh commanded every son born to the Hebrews to be thrown into the Nile, but the daughters were allowed to live. When Moses was born, his mother hid him for three months. The Bible states in Hebrews 11:23 (ESV) that he was hidden by his mother by faith because the child was beautiful and she was not afraid of the king's edict. Faith without works is dead, as we are told in James 2:14-22. In the midst of the turmoil, she made a desperate decision to release Moses into the Nile River in a woven basket.

What happened next was nothing short of miraculous.

> Now the daughter of Pharaoh came down to bathe at the river, while her young women walked beside the river. She saw the basket among the reeds and sent her servant woman, and she took it. When she opened it,

she saw the child, and behold, the baby was crying. She took pity on him and said, "This is one of the Hebrews' children." Then his sister said to Pharaoh's daughter, "Shall I go and call you a nurse from the Hebrew women to nurse the child for you?" And Pharaoh's daughter said to her, "Go." So the girl went and called the child's mother. And Pharaoh's daughter said to her, "Take this child away and nurse him for me, and I will give you your wages." So the woman took the child and nursed him. When the child grew older, she brought him to Pharaoh's daughter, and he became her son. She named him Moses, "Because," she said, "I drew him out of the water."

Exodus 2:5-10 (ESV)

For forty years, Moses lived as a son to Pharaoh's daughter and as a prince in the Egyptian court. According to Acts 7:22 (ESV), *"Moses was educated in all the wisdom and culture of the Egyptians, and he was mighty (powerful) in his speech and deeds."* We should note some important points from this Scripture alone.

Moses wasn't merely educated as the common people were; he was given the best education in the world at that time—an education was thorough and extensive, one befitting a future ruler of Egypt (as the plan most likely was).

According to Charles F. Aling in his book *Egypt and Bible History*, Moses's education came from the officials of the land. He received academic instruction as well as physical instruction. Moses was educated in hieroglyphic and hieratic scripts, spending endless hours copying and memorizing voluminous lists of words and names. He also studied foreign languages of the Near Eastern world. This probably included Akkadian (the language of Babylonia) and the Canaanite dialects. He also studied math, but the academic subject considered of primary importance was rhetoric. The Egyptians highly valued the ability to speak well in public, and accordingly, it received heavy attention during the years of formal education. Rhetoric in Egypt comprised not only public speaking but also proper style in writing.[14]

Being raised as a prince in Egypt meant that Moses was informed of the world in which he lived. He understood Egypt's culture, politics, and history. He was trained as a leader and military warrior. Ironically, while the Egyptians intended his education to be put to their use, it was really ordained by God in preparation for his role in delivering God's people from slavery and beginning a new nation, much to the detriment of Egypt. The new nation would be no ordinary nation, but one set apart to serve and honor the living God.

Of course, challenges abounded. The people of Israel would have to be taught to conduct their lives as free people. A new government would have to be established. God through Moses would have to establish new laws, rules, and ordinances. This was a monumental task, but not one given to Moses in a void of knowledge. Laws and ordinances that Moses could rely upon were established as far back as Abraham. With God's leading, Moses was able to improve upon them. When Moses wrote the biblical law, several cuneiform codes were being practiced throughout the Near East. According to Westbrook and Wells in their book *Everyday Law in Biblical Israel*, seven law codes have been recovered to date:

- The Laws of Ur-Namma (LU), from the city of Ur in southern Mesopotamia, written in Sumerian and dating to around 2100 BC.
- The Laws of Lipit-Ishtar (LL), from the city of Isin in

southern Mesopotamia, written in Sumerian and dating to around 1900 BC.

- The Laws of Eshnunna (LE), from a city of that name in northern Mesopotamia, written in Akkadian and dating to around 1800 BC.
- The Laws of Hammurabi (LH), from the city of Babylon, written in Arcadian and dating to around 1750 BC.
- The Middle Assyrian Laws (NBL), from the city of Sippar in central Mesopotamia, written in Akkadian and dating to the seventh century BC.
- The Neo-Babylonian Laws (NBL) from the city of Sippar in central Mesopotamia, written in Akkadian and dating to the seventh century BC.
- The Hittite Laws (HL), from Anatolia, written in cuneiform script in Hittite and dating between the sixteenth and twelfth centuries BC. [15]

All of these codes have similar laws and precepts. They extend through thousands of years and multiple cultures, yet the underlying principles of these laws remain the same. As stated in *Everyday Law,*

> The biblical laws fit into this pattern. They are for the most part casuistic in form and contain many cases found in other law codes. The parallels between the biblical and cuneiform laws are the closest that any literary genre in the Bible has with an external source. They demonstrate that the clusters of everyday law are not a modern construction, but must already had had some independent existence in antiquity.[16]

What does this tell us about the laws of Moses? When Moses brought the people of Israel out of bondage, he issued laws and decrees that they were to live by. Some laws were already established and didn't need to be altered. Others were given by divine inspiration, mandated by God through Moses. For example, consider this law of Hammurabi from the city of Babylon:

> If a man destroy the eye of another man, they shall destroy his eye. If one break a man's bone, they shall break his bone. If one destroy the eye of a freeman or break the bone of a freeman he shall pay one mana of silver. If one destroy the eye of a man's slave or break a bone of a man's slave he shall pay one-half his price. If a man knock out a tooth of a man of his own rank, they shall knock out his tooth. If one knock out a tooth of a freeman, he shall pay one-third mana of silver.[17]

This is the same law from Moses in Exodus 21:24(ESV) which states, "*Eye for eye, tooth for tooth.*" Some say that Moses just copied the Hammurabi law. Others say that Moses wasn't even aware of the Hammurabi law. What is the truth?

With the education and training that Moses had as a prince of Egypt, he must have been fully aware of these other law codes, but to say he just copied them with no contemplation cannot be true either. In everything he did, he sought the wisdom of God. Most likely, he decided that there were some established laws that could be kept, and that others that required change. Further, it's likely that the people he was leading were familiar with some of the laws. Would it not be prudent, then, to lead them with codes that they knew?

Of course, other laws of Moses represented a radical change. The first two commandments of the famous Ten Commandments display the fact that God was separating His people for Himself by demanding they worship Him and Him alone, having no other gods before Him. The people of Israel had just come out of severe bondage in Egypt. They had a difficult time even grasping that God alone needed to be worshiped. Indeed, if that weren't the case, they wouldn't have made a golden calf to worship while Moses was away to receive the very laws they were breaking. Obviously, they needed the additional laws.

As a lawgiver, Moses possessed godly wisdom to lead the people. As such, he used some existing laws—those based on universal principles—that the people of Israel already knew. He then skillfully integrated these with a new order of laws that God gave him. These laws established a holy and consecrated relationship with God.

The law code compiled by Moses included laws pertaining to people's daily lives. It covered damage to property, loss of property, injury, homicide, family law, hygiene, and sexual offenses. In forming this code, Moses faced the same challenges that lawgivers face today: Possessed of a deep sense of justice and understanding of their culture, how do they create laws in a way that benefits society as a whole while preserving individual liberty?

Today in the United States, thousands of laws exist. Most are good laws, though some lack common sense, and a few border on lunacy. Those who desire to be in government, particularly in the legislative branch, must apply prayer and sound principles to change unjust laws and create good laws—laws that allows us to live in peace and worship God in freedom.

The Government and Its People

6

Deborah

At the time of Judges, the nation of Israel was in flux. Moses had led them out of Egypt and through the desert, losing an entire generation of unbelieving ex-slaves in the process. Joshua had brought Israel into the Promised Land, but he had failed to complete his mission of total conquest, thus Israel was inhabiting an region influenced by Canaanite politics and religion. The 12 tribes of Israel were also split geographically by Canaanite cities that were not taken in the conquest, causing a deep divide in the nation. Because of this, the tribes struggled to unite as one nation in times of oppression and threats from foreign nations. In fact, some tribes were completely left to fend for themselves.

Moses and Joshua had been powerful, skilled leaders. Unfortunately, the tribes did not have a key leader at the time of Judges. Scripture states in Judges 3 that the Lord allowed foreign nations to test Israel so the Israelites would learn the art of war. Inevitably, the culture of these nations became integrated into everyday life for the people of Israel, so much so that they married the daughters of these foreign nations, gave their own daughters to marry other nations' sons, and ultimately served their gods.

This began a cycle where the people of Israel would abandon

the Lord completely and commit apostasy with other nations. Then these nations that they turned to would rule and oppress them. Israel would then cry out to the Lord for deliverance. And the Lord would raise up deliverers to save them. At this time in history, these deliverers were called judges.

Interestingly, no judge presided in the office of judge except for one: Deborah.

Like Moses, Deborah filled more than just one role. She was a judge, military leader, and prophetess. Her name means "Bee," and Scripture says that she was the "wife of Lapidot." The Hebrew words are *eset lapidot*, which could also mean "woman of torches." Given Deborah's role in history, this author believes the term means "fiery woman." She was a charismatic, industrious woman, and whether she was married or not does not take away from her judicial and political role in Israel.

In the song of Deborah, a lengthy poem found in Judges 5, we can read of Israel's condition before Deborah rose in power.

> *In the days of Shamgar son of Anath,*
> *in the days of Jael, the highways were abandoned;*
> *travelers took to winding paths.*
> *Villagers in Israel would not fight;*
> *they held back until I, Deborah, arose,*
> *until I arose, a mother in Israel.*

Judges 5:6-7

According to Cundall and Morris, the word "highways" should be read as "caravans," meaning that commercial trading was impossible, and those who had to travel did so on the less-frequented routes to avoid being molested.[18]

"*The villagers would not fight,*" implies that no one was actively involved in the protection and oversight of the people and their activities.

In the midst of this trouble, Deborah came on the scene as a leader and judge. She sat under the Palm of Deborah and made judicial decisions for the people, most likely the same kind of decisions that Moses made when he sat as judge, and later, as elders would do at the gates of Jersualem. [Initially, Moses sat with complete judicial authority, but then delegated his authority to able men from the elders and officials in the tribes (Deuteronomy 1:9-17 ESV)].

At the time of Judges, the tribes of Israel were loosely bound together, and they did not have any specific courts or magistrates to settle their disputes. The Bible says that every person did what was right in his own eyes. How Deborah came to be judge is not mentioned. The Bible does not give much description or background of her life. It seems, however, that when disputes arose that the people could not settle between themselves, they came to her for judgment.

Deborah arose as *"a mother in Israel."* Another scripture coincides with the term *"mother in Israel."*

> *They used to say in former times, 'Let them but ask counsel at Abel,' and so they settled a matter. I'm one of those who are peaceable and faithful in Israel. You seek to destroy a city that is a mother in Israel. Why will you swallow up the heritage of the Lord?*
>
> 2 Samuel 20:18-19(ESV)

According to Susan Ackerman, Abel-Beth-Ma`acah was called *"a mother in Israel"* because people went there to ask counsel and settled their disputes.[19] What kind of decisions and disputes did Deborah settle? Likely, they would have been the casuistic laws that were followed universally in the whole region. As mentioned in an earlier chapter, casuistic laws affected people's everyday lives—damage to property, loss of property, injury, homicide, family law, and more. These contrasted with Apodictic laws which referred to divine commands of irrefutable truth.

Deborah was gifted with wisdom and authority to release justice as a mother to Israel. This mother symbol speaks of mercy and impartiality, as in a judge who would decide with great care and concern for both the plaintiff and defendant. In Isaiah 1, the Lord was displeased with Israel's existing rulers and judges because they loved bribes and did not defend the fatherless and widow. In verse 26, the Lord promises to restore the judges once again.

> *Your rulers are rebels,*
> *partners with thieves;*
> *they all love bribes*
> *and chase after gifts.*
> *They do not defend the cause of the fatherless;*
> *the widow's case does not come before them.*

Isaiah 1:33

Today, more than ever, we need judges who will decide according to basic humane principles that are fair to all; judges who will not favor people with money or power, or succumb to political pressure, but who will judge with courage and a good conscience so that humankind will not suffer when corruption is released. When corruption happens, it places a burden of despair on people, one that is incapable of being lifted without judges ruling according to basic, natural laws of justice, common sense, and fairness.

7

David and Solomon

O f all the characters in the Bible who were called of God to participate in civil government, the rule of King David and then his son Solomon marks the end of one era and the beginning of another era—that of God's eternal government. God promised that He would establish a kingdom through David, and that his throne would last forever.

> Your house and your kingdom will endure forever before me; your throne will be established forever.

> 2 Samuel 7:16

Of course, when Nathan the prophet gave this prophetic promise, who could have imagined that the kingdom of God's government and rule would include people from every nation of the world? God chose David to begin His eternal kingdom, and He had a specific reason for doing so. In Acts, Paul explains that David was chosen because he was a man after God's heart, someone who would do God's will.

> After removing Saul, he made David their king. God testified concerning him: "I have found David son of Jesse, a man after my own heart; he will do everything I want him to do."

Acts 13:22

The Scriptures say over and over that David's heart was perfect before God. One of the definitions for perfect is "whole." David served God with his whole heart; it was never divided, and he never served other religious gods or forms. He did make mistakes—some major mistakes—but he repented and God forgave him.

A few years ago, I was watching a Washington correspondent talk about his experiences interviewing several past presidents of the United States. One of his observations was that the men who became president didn't just arrive from out of nowhere. He said that there was a story, a background, and a process through which these men became president. Indeed, it was their stories that made their lives compelling.

David did not become king the day, or even the year, that God appointed him. It took several years of trials, testing, and suffering before he would be qualified to rule. He wasn't automatically handed the authority and the power of kingship. His character was formed and his patience tried. Under God's tutelage, David's process journey to rulership was deep and thorough.

Reading David's life story, it can seem that David's preparation was the exact opposite of what he was promised. David himself could not perceive the fullness to which he was called. He was chosen to be the king of Israel, and his son Solomon was eventually chosen to succeed him, but the Bible also reveals the promise of an eternal kingdom.

> *His seed shall endure forever, and his throne as the sun before Me [God], and it shall be established forever as the moon as a faithful witness in heaven.*

Psalm 89:36-37 (ASV)

But what did that mean to David at the time? Did he see Israel established as a nation forever and ever on the earth? Did he know that God Himself would come in the flesh through his lineage and die for the sin of all humankind? Did he know that the Son of God would also be referred to as the Son of David? Did he know that more pages would be written about him on the earth than any other person who lived besides Christ Jesus?

David's extensive preparation was for both a temporal government and an eternal government. Our Lord Jesus came from the lineage of David, according to the promise that his seed would be established forever. David was chosen beforehand to walk in the work to which he was called. Those of us in Christ are also called to good works and to walk in them.

> *For we are his workmanship, created in Christ Jesus*
> *for good works, which God prepared beforehand, that*
> *we should walk in them.*

> Ephesians 2:10 (ESV)

Faithfulness and perseverance are the keys. The reward is rulership. In the parable of the talents (Luke 19:11-27), we see that the servants that remained faithful to the Lord until He returned received cities to govern. God rewards with increased responsibility and authority to govern. It is an honor to rule governmentally. It is a reward.

Some Christians have more of a slave mentality than a ruler mentality. They think they are humble and pure by not being involved in politics and government, that even the Lord Himself would caution them to back away. These people are wrong. Our earthly life is preparation for eternity. We may not be called to the same vocations and occupations that we knew in this life, but we are called to be faithful and to rule over that which He has entrusted to us for eternity.

Like David, we don't see all that God is preparing for us for, but we know according to Scripture that we are destined to rule with Christ Jesus if we continue strong in the faith and remain obedient to His will for our lives.

Solomon was given the kingdom by his father. David prepared everything for his son to continue the reign, knowing it would be a daunting task. Solomon was wise enough to ask God for wisdom, knowing from his father's instruction that he couldn't reign without it.

> *Hear, my son, your father's instruction,*
> *and forsake not your mother's teaching,*
> *for they are a graceful garland for your head*
> *and pendants for your neck.*
>
> Proverbs 1:8-9 (ESV)

Note the source of Solomon's teaching. He was admonished to receive both the instruction from his father and the teaching from his mother. Yes, Solomon was instructed from a young age in how to rule, yet when his time came, he cried out to the Lord for wisdom.

> *By me kings reign, and rulers decree what is just; by*
> *me princes rule, and nobles, all who govern justly.*
>
> Proverbs 8:15-16 (ESV)

This is the essence of administering justice.

What is justice? The basic definition is "the administering of deserved punishment or reward." The Oxford English Dictionary defines the just person as one who typically "does what is morally right" and is disposed to "giving everyone his or her due," offering the word "fair" as a synonym.[20] So justice is doing what is fair and right to everyone in society.

This means that everyone should receive the rewards that

are due from their work and responsibilities. Therefore, injustice happens when men try to occupy positions in things they are not prepared for, appropriating rewards to which they are not entitled. Laws are created to give everyone their due.

This principle of giving everyone their due is administered through different types of justice. Differing worldviews and opinions exist regarding what is truly justice and how it should be applied. Further, this subject has been at the core of ethics and morality debates for centuries. Justice has several layers; therefore, it makes sense that people's sense of justice differs depending on the individual case and circumstances.

Justice must be based on what is fair, what is right, and what is moral. And even though the core remains the same, there are different applications of justice, primarily: distribution, retribution, and restoration.

Distribution can also be called social justice because it deals with economics and the goods and services people receive. Many believe that goods should be distributed simply by need. Others believe that other criteria should govern, such as earning as the right to possession.

Retribution is corrective justice. This involves punishing a person for crimes against humanity. This justice involves making clear decisions and ensuring that the punishment meets the crime. For instance, we wouldn't stone someone to death for stealing from a cash register.

Restitution is also called restorative justice, and it presents itself in various ways. Fundamentally, it means that the person who has been injured or robbed should be compensated for their loss. Determining what is fair compensation is an aspect of this justice.

Justice is not just about obeying the laws, however. Historically, the poor are afflicted and taken advantage of by the rich. We see this in literature, including the writings of Charles Dickens, which often illustrate what Scripture is trying to convey. The poor are shown no mercy because of the greed of their overseers. Hence the scriptural admonishment.

> *Rob not the poor, because he is poor, or crush the afflicted at the gate*
>
> Proverbs 22:22
>
> *For I know your manifold transgressions and your mighty sins: they afflict the just, they take a bribe, and they turn aside the poor in the gate from their right.*
>
> Amos 5:12 (KJV)

According to the Bible, the poor have rights, but they do not have a right to be wicked, lazy, or covetous. According to the parable of the talents (Luke 19:12-26), the man who only had one pound and did nothing with it, had that pound taken away and given to the man with ten pounds. Covetousness is not against the law of civil court, but it is addressed by the tenth commandment according to the Law of Moses.

> *"You shall not covet your neighbor's house. You shall not covet your neighbor's wife, or his male or female servant, his ox or donkey, or anything that belongs to your neighbor."*
>
> Exodus 20:17

This admonishment against covetousness is further echoed throughout the New Testament, giving credence to the fact that we do have natural rights in society.

So, what does it mean to covet? According to Dictionary.com, "covet" means, "to desire wrongfully, inordinately, or without due regard for the rights of others."[21] According to the Bible, a person is not allowed to covet that which they have no right to possess. The positive benefit of this is that people have a right to their own things and relationships without fear of someone else misappropriating them. This principle is deeply embedded in our consciousness and our hearts, as borne out by the proclamation of the prophet Amos.

> *But let justice roll down like waters, and righteousness*
> *like an ever-flowing stream.*
>
> Amos 5:24 (ESV)

Justice flows from the heart of God.

Solomon asked for wisdom to rule, and it was given to him. In Proverbs, he detailed how people should live out their lives in order, peace, and harmony. Solomon was not given a set of laws to rule by, but a heart of wisdom and understanding for how people should live and conduct their affairs.

Whether it is a city mayor, a state governor, or the President of the United States, if the ruler is God-fearing, they can ask for wisdom and receive discernment on how to apply justice. Consider the promise of God embedded in James.

> *If any of you lacks wisdom, let him ask God, who*
> *gives generously to all without reproach, and it will*
> *be given him.*
>
> James 1:5 (ESV)

The most efficient, just, and fair leaders will be those leading and discerning with godly wisdom—the same wisdom given to King Solomon.

The Government and Its People

8

Elijah

Elijah was a fiery prophet sent by God to confront a feckless King Ahab. Historically, the facts are that King Ahab was a powerful ruler in the Near East. He was the son of Omri, the king of Israel who established Samaria as his capital. Omri was a major figure in international affairs, a strong military commander and developer of enormous building projects. In the book *The Bible Unearthed,* by Finkelstein and Silberman, the authors write:

> Samaria was the most grandiose architectural manifestation of the rule of Omri and Ahab. It was a royal acropolis of five acres that can be compared in audacity and extravagance (though perhaps not in size) only to the work that Herod the Great carried out almost a millennium later on the Temple Mount in Jerusalem.[22]

Ahab continued to expand the dynasty his father began. He operated a huge army; he conducted large building projects and built cities. Then he married Jezebel, the daughter of the Phoenician king Ethbaal. According to Finkelstein and Silberman, marrying Jezebel could have been looked upon historically as a brilliant stroke of international diplomacy.[23] It was not a brilliant action, however, according to the writers of the Hebrew Bible.

> *And Ahab the son of Omri did evil in the sight of the Lord, more than all who were before him. And as if it had been a light thing for him to walk in the sins of Jeroboam the son of Nebat, he took for his wife Jezebel the daughter of Ethbaal king of the Sidonians, and went and served Baal and worshiped him. He erected an altar for Baal in the house of Baal, which he built in Samaria. And Ahab made an Asherah. Ahab did more to provoke the Lord, the God of Israel, to anger than all the kings of Israel who were before him.*
>
> 1 Kings 16:30-33 (ESV)

It's never a good thing to have written that a king did more to provoke the Lord to anger more than all the other kings before him. All the grandeur of the Israelite kingdom meant nothing compared to the national sins being committed in the capital of Samaria. The Lord did not take lightly this insurrection to His commands and precepts. Because of Ahab's pride in his prominence and achievements, he wasn't going to be corrected by just a prophetic word from a prophet. He would have to be confronted with acts of judgment. To that end, the Lord called the prophet Elijah to defy Ahab and Jezebel. This was no small task.

Elijah was called to confront one of the most powerful kings of Israel. In so doing, he was facing head-on the wickedness of an entire nation. Elijah was a prophet of fire whose name means "Yahweh is God." He was anointed with signs, wonders, and miracles to confront the deep inroads that Baal worship had made in the hearts of God's people. The people of God were being deceived by Baal's prophets. Baal was worshiped as the king of the gods as well as the god of storms and fertility. Because these were vital elements to the everyday lives of Israel, Baal worship played an active role in the people's existence.

Elijah was appointed by God to expose the lies perpetrated by the prophets of Baal who said that Yahweh was just another God. Every act of Elijah was ordained to challenge people's faith in Baal. He confronted them, stating that they were vacillating between two beliefs—Baal and the Lord God. Elijah was ordained to show that Baal was nothing compared to God.

Elijah, through the power of God, confronted Baal worship in the areas of its supposed authority—the weather and growing seasons. Elijah declared a drought on the land. There was no rain for three years and the famine in Samaria was severe. God took away the rain to display His authority over the elements. This left Ahab in a desperate situation. Then God raised the stakes.

After many days the word of the Lord came to Elijah, in the third year, saying, "Go, show yourself to Ahab, and I will send rain upon the earth."

1 Kings 18:1

At first glance, this might appear to be good news to Ahab— the drought is over. But remember, the battle was not over rain in Israel, but to settle the question of who would reign in Israel. Elijah opposed Ahab directly with the authority of the Lord God, and when he declared the drought over, he did so with the same authority.

Elijah was displaying governmental authority. He was a governmental prophet called to rebuke the highest form of government. This authority came with power and went much further than challenging the influence of a local demonic religion. God, through Elijah, was extending the fight to the hearts and minds of the people.

When Ahab saw Elijah, Ahab said to him, "Is it you, you troubler of Israel?" And he answered, "I have not troubled Israel, but you have, and your father's house, because you have abandoned the commandments of the Lord and followed the Baals. Now therefore send and gather all Israel to me at Mount Carmel, and the 450 prophets of Baal and the 400 prophets of Asherah, who eat at Jezebel's table."

So Ahab sent to all the people of Israel and gathered the prophets together at Mount Carmel. And Elijah came near to all the people and said, "How long will you go limping between two different opinions? If the Lord is God, follow him; but if Baal, then follow him." And the people did not answer him a word.

1 King 18:17-21 (ESV)

Elijah challenged the prophets of Baal with power and fire in one of the greatest spectacles recorded in Scripture. Both sides prepared a sacrifice upon an altar, and the god who answered by consuming the sacrifice with fire would be God in all the land.

The prophets of Baal went first, crying out all day, cutting themselves with swords and pleading to their god, but there was no answer from Baal. Then toward evening, it was Elijah's turn. But before he asked God to consume his sacrifice, he ordered his alter to be drenched with water, not once but three times. Then he prayed.

And at the time of the offering of the oblation, Elijah the prophet came near and said, "O Lord, God of Abraham, Isaac, and Israel, let it be known this day that you are God in Israel, and that I am your servant, and that I have done all these things at your word.

*Answer me, O Lord, answer me, that this people may
know that you, O Lord, are God, and that you have
turned their hearts back."*

Then God answered Elijah's prayer.

*Then the fire of the Lord fell and consumed the burnt
offering and the wood and the stones and the dust,
and licked up the water that was in the trench.*

1 King 18:36-38 (ESV)

There were no more questions in the hearts of the people. The Lord was God, and now, it was judgement time.

*And when all the people saw it, they fell on their faces
and said, "The Lord, he is God; the Lord, he is God."
And Elijah said to them, "Seize the prophets of Baal;
let not one of them escape." And they seized them.
And Elijah brought them down to the brook Kishon
and slaughtered them there.*

1 King 18:39-40 (ESV)

That day at Mount Carmel was a day of judgment, cleansing, restoration, and appearing. One lone prophet of God stood against 450 prophets of Baal and won. This was no easy task. The prophets of Baal served at Jezebel's table. They were high and powerful in the government of Ahab. They were not only spiritual prophets but political prophets as well, active in the community and governmental affairs. They led the people of Israel astray and kept them in deep darkness, causing them to turn away from the one true God.

Yet, even though this display of God's power was a decisive victory that turned the Lord's people back to Him, it did not fully root out the corruption in the government. Elijah thought there had been a thorough cleansing of the Baal culture, but to his astonishment, it didn't touch the heart of Jezebel. The defeat of Baal only enraged Jezebel more, causing her to threaten Elijah's life. He ran into a cave where he began to question God.

Elijah, despite his great power from God, became so discouraged that he thought he was only faithful believer left in Israel. However, God corrected him saying:

> *"Yet I will leave seven thousand in Israel, all the knees that have not bowed to Baal, and every mouth that has not kissed him."*
>
> 1 Kings 19:18 (ESV)

God showed Elijah that feeling isolated and being isolated are two different things. Eventually, because of Elijah's faithfulness to God, Jezebel was dealt a final blow, bringing to an end the heart of Baal worship in Israel.

This victory could not have come had Elijah not exercised his God-given authority to challenge the government. We have similar authority today. Christians living in the United States also have authority to challenge their government. Our authority comes from God as we worship and obey the Lord, and that same authority flows down to the foundation of our government.

> *Governments are instituted among men, deriving their just powers from the consent of the governed.*
>
> The Declaration of Independence

Our authority begins with the Constitution of the United States, and includes the first 10 amendments to the Constitution, commonly called The Bill of Rights.

The Bill of Rights was established to safeguard individual's rights by placing limits on the power of the government. The very first line in the first amendment is this:

> *Congress shall make no law respecting an*

establishment of religion, or prohibiting the free exercise thereof.

Christians living in the United States have the freedom to worship God openly. It is the law of the land. And because of that, we can stand up for our beliefs and defend them when called upon to do so.

Ecclesiastes 3:7 states that there is a time to keep silent and a time to speak. Sometimes our governmental leaders need to be openly rebuked when they begin to sway public opinion against our religious freedom and even persecute Christians for their deeply held beliefs. The law is on our side, and that is the grace of God.

In this world, because of the media, Internet, and diverse political persuasions, it's easy to believe that just a few people still follow after God's heart. But in reality, there are many, and we are growing in number all over the world. The Lord will continue to raise up prophets of fire and rain to declare to the whole world and its governments that "the Lord, He is God!"

9

Daniel

The prophet Daniel declared to King Nebuchadnezzar of Babylon that God rules the kingdom of men and gives it to whomever He wills, even the lowest of men.

> *"The Most High is sovereign over all kingdoms on earth and gives them to anyone he wishes and sets over them the lowliest of people."*

Daniel 4:17 (ESV)

At this time in Israel's history, the Jews were captives of Babylon. Because of the sins and apostasy of God's people, they had been overthrown and enslaved by the Babylonians. They no longer had the privilege of being a nation. Instead, they had to learn to live again in a foreign land with a different religion and culture. Chaldean culture was widespread among the Babylonians. It was from this culture that the Babylonians perfected the art of magic. This included the activities of magicians, sorcerers, and enchanters, and the use of omens, incantations, astrology and other occult practices to tell the future and search for hidden mysteries.

King Nebuchadnezzar ordered his court official—the master of the eunuchs—to bring the most promising youths from the exiled Jews to be trained in his court. These youths were to be of royal seed and nobility. The Bible states that they were without blemish, well favored, skillful in all wisdom, endued with knowledge and understanding of science. The master of the eunuchs was directed to teach the youths the language and culture of the Chaldeans. Four of the chosen were Daniel, Hananiah, Mishael, and Azariah.

Joyce G. Baldwin writes that the study of Babylonian literature was a completely alien world to these young men of Judah.

> *According to the Sumerians and Babylonians, two classes of persons inhabited the universe: the human race and the gods. Pre-eminence belonged to the gods, though they were not all equal. At the lower end of the divine scale came a host of minor deities and demons, while a trinity of great gods—Anu, Enlil, and Ea—stood at their head. A modern scholar will observe that many of these gods are personifications of parts or aspects of nature. The sun and moon gods are obvious examples.* [24]

Because of the king's order, Daniel and his companions were brought into the highest level of Babylonian government. As part of their training, their names were changed from Hebrew names to Babylonian names. Further, they were expected to serve and obey the king and his laws, learn the culture of Babylon, and live within the prevailing culture.

In conforming to the king's wishes while staying true to God, Daniel serves as an example of how Christians should live in this present world. Most countries today are led by secular governments. These governments have no allegiance to Jesus Christ or His work. Instead, they look to themselves for the solutions to difficult problems in leading their nations. Still, if they are good governments, they will follow godly principles even if they do not acknowledge the source of these principles.

Daniel

Daniel and his companions were endowed with godly wisdom, and it raised their stature in the Babylonian kingdom. Daniel was able to be useful to a secular government while still maintaining his firm faith in God. Notice that during his training in Babylonian culture, Daniel and his companions refused to eat at the king's table. This was no small thing. It could have cost the life of the official who was in charge of their wellbeing.

Scripture states that eating at the king's table would have defiled Daniel. This defilement was not necessarily dietary because, as Baldwin points out:

> *All food in Babylon and Assyria was ritually unclean, and from that there was not escape. Daniel 11:26 (ESV) provides more light as to why he refused to eat at the king's table. 'Even those who eat his rich food shall be his undoing.' By eastern standards to share a meal was to commit oneself to friendship; it was of covenant significance."*[25]

In the East, partaking at one's table is deeply relational. Still, Daniel had not arrived at the king's court by his own volition. He was taken as a servant. Therefore, he was not there to commit his heart to the king in friendship through sharing a meal; he was there to serve and represent God to a godless nation. The Lord guided Daniel and protected him in these daily decisions. Daniel learned to walk out his life before the Lord while being established in a secular government.

The Bible states that, because of the obedience of Daniel and his companions:

> *The king had appointed for them to be brought before him, and the king conversed with them, and among them none were found like Daniel and his*

companions. The king found them ten times wiser than all the magicians and enchanters who wherein his whole realm.

Daniel 1:19-20 (AMP)

Daniel and his friends stood out and apart from the rest of the king's court. They were given wisdom and spiritual gifts to serve the king with depth and accuracy. They excelled in their discernment and interpretation of dreams and visions because the Lord positioned them and equipped them to perform their duties to the king.

Daniel served as an adviser to four kings: Nebuchadnezzar, Belshazzar, Darius, and Cyrus. The Lord displayed His knowledge, power, and protection while administering His judgment and decrees differently to each king.

Here are some ways that God showed himself as the ultimate ruler of all mankind:

1. Nebuchadnezzar had a dream that troubled him. He called upon his cabinet of magicians, enchanters, soothsayers, sorcerers, and diviners to tell the king what he had dreamed and what it meant. They could not tell the king and stated that no man on earth could show the king his dream. Nebuchadnezzar then decreed that the wise men of Babylon were to be killed. This included Daniel and his companions. Daniel asked the king for some time and then he and his companions sought the Lord in prayer, and the dream with the interpretation was given to Daniel. Daniel cried out of his heart,

"[The Lord] reveals deep and hidden things;
he knows what is in the darkness,
and the light dwells with him.
To you, O God of my fathers,

Daniel

I give thanks and praise,
for you have given me wisdom and might,
and have now made known to me what we asked of you,
for you have made known to us the king's matter."

Daniel 2:22-23 (ESV)

2. Nebuchadnezzar made an image of gold. Then he sent for every government official and cabinet member to be at the dedication of his golden image. He asked for the satraps, deputies, governors, judges, chief stargazers, treasurers, counselors, sheriffs, lawyers, and every other chief official. It was one important national event! He commanded that when the people heard the sound of music, they were to fall down and worship the golden image. Whoever did not bow down and worship would be cast into a fiery furnace that very hour (Daniel 3). Of course, Daniel's three friends refused to bow to the golden image. This was reported to the king, and it enraged him. He confronted Shadrach, Meshach, and Abednego, and threatened to cast them into the fiery furnace, asking them what god could deliver them out of his hands. They responded by saying that God will deliver them, but even if He didn't, they would not serve the king's gods or worship his golden image.

In the end, these three men of God were delivered out of the fiery furnace without even a whiff of smoke on them, causing a heathen king to bless and praise the living God.

3. Belshazzar became king after Nebuchadnezzar. By that time, Daniel had been made chief of the magicians, enchanters, soothsayers, and astrologers because he was known to have an excellent spirit, knowledge, and understanding to interpret dreams, clarify riddles, and solve knotty problems. When he was called upon by the king to read the famous "writing on the wall,"

Daniel declared to the king that the end of his kingdom was at hand. The king was slain that very night.

4. Darius became king and promoted Daniel to a high governmental office, being chosen to share rule over the entire kingdom with two other officials. But Daniel became so distinguished above the other officials that the king planned to set him over the whole kingdom. That stirred up a jealous spirit among the other two officials, and they conspired against Daniel, coming against his personal prayer life and intercession. King Darius had issued an edict requiring that all people pray to him, and to him alone, for thirty days. Daniel refused and was thrown into the lions' den for praying to his god. And yet, God delivered Daniel, causing Darius to make a decree stating that the Lord is the living God, enduring forever, that His kingdom shall never be destroyed, and his dominion shall never end. The end of Daniel 6 states that Daniel prospered during the reigns of Darius and Cyrus the Persian.

Daniel and his companions worked and lived among those whose beliefs, morals, and values were not only different, but were often blasphemous to a holy God. And yet, this was by God's design. The Lord could have supplied a quiet community for His servants to live in—a hiding place far from the center of current political events and the upheavals of changing times. Instead, the Lord God placed his chosen servants in the middle of the culture where He protected, promoted, and prospered them. It was there that they thrived, demonstrated that it's not the external environment that makes the difference in a believer's life, but whether they are in the will of God.

Daniel was in the highest levels of government and thrived in his relationship with God. Indeed, not only did he survive, but his spiritual life flourished. His kingdom prophecies are still being studied today.

Daniel and his friends serve as examples of how we can serve God in a secular government. They were given solutions and shown "the writing on the wall" while refusing to bow or worship any other gods. They drew their lines and the Lord kept them safe and prosperous, proving over and over again that He was the only true living God, now and forever.

The Government and Its People

10

Esther

The book of Esther is a fascinating story that stands out differently than the books of Daniel and Nehemiah with regards to the attitude, convictions, and worldview of the Jewish people. Esther is unique among the books of the Bible because God is not mentioned and there is no reference to His laws. In the story, Esther and her uncle Mordecai were living in Sousa fifty years after Cyrus the king decreed that the Jewish people could go back to Jerusalem to rebuild the temple. King Xerxes, also known as Ahasuerus, took the throne in 486 BC. He was the second Persian king following Darius the Mede.

For years, the famous declaration from Esther, *"And who knows whether you have not come to the kingdom for such a time as this?"* (Esther 4:14), has been quoted and glamorized in sermons and prophetic utterances. Those words mean, of course, that Esther was chosen by God for a special time and place in history. Yet, a closer look at the circumstances that caused Esther to become queen is baffling and questionable.

Culturally and politically, Esther and Mordecai were rooted in Susa. If that wasn't the case, they would have easily relocated to Jerusalem at some point in their personal timeline. Apparently, they were comfortable and established in the Persian environment. Further, Mordecai was not an invisible citizen in Susa; he was likely from nobility and well known in both the Jewish community and the Persian government. How do we know this? Because Mordecai sat at the gate of the palace (Esther 2:21 ESV).

According to jewishbible.org:

> The name Mordecai is mentioned 58 times in the Book of Esther. Five times he is referred to as Mordecai Hayehudi, usually translated, "Mordecai the Jew." Perhaps a better translation might be "the Jewish Judge," for all five times refer to Mordecai in an official capacity... The phrase "sitting at the gate" is a common Biblical way of referring to a member of the court of justice... Bible critics agree with classical Jewish commentators that the phrase "gates" usually means courts.

> The Talmud reports the tradition that Mordecai was the head of the Jewish court. Since it was usually Persian policy, except during times of religious persecution, to give considerable independence to ethnic minorities, it would have been probable for King Ahasuerus or his predecessor to have appointed or affirmed the appointment of a Jewish judge, possibly giving him an official title or at least a name as Belshazzar gave Daniel.[26]

Mordecai had so much influence in the Persian government that he was able to get information to King Xerxes about a secret plot to assassinate him, warning the king in time and saving his life. Later, as an established government official, Mordecai not only persuaded Esther to prepare herself with hundreds of other virgins to come before the king, but was also able to secretly get her through the process without any of the Persian officials' knowledge of her Jewish origins.

At first glance, this seems like a shrewd move, which in fact it is, but take note that Mordecai insisted on deception to get Esther through the courts of the king. He lied and Esther lied. Not only is lying involved, but also the complete dismissal of the law of Moses and God's covenant. The law explicitly states that God's people were not to engage in marriage outside the Jewish faith. In the instance of Mordecai and Esther, Mordecai brought his own relative in to engage in a sexual union with a pagan king before there was any hint of marriage.

Esther submitted to Mordecai as her father and elder, but she also showed no resistance in any capacity in preparing herself to sleep with a pagan king. In fact, the goal was to so please him in bed that she might become queen instead of Vashti. To put this plainly, this would be like a Christian parent instructing their virgin daughter or son to deny they are a Christian and have sexual intercourse with a mayor, governor, congressperson, or president in order to gain access to these high-level positions. This is unthinkable for a Christian. It seems that Mordecai was maneuvering and manipulating his niece, advising her in such a way that would benefit his goals and aspirations.

And yet this is precisely how God saved the Jewish people.

The story of Esther displays more concern about politics and nationalism than about the observance of God's laws. This brings to mind Paul's observation that *"now we see through a glass, darkly"* (1 Corinthians 13:12 KJV). God and his Word give entrance to light and truth. So before we judge Mordecai and Esther, recall that others in the Bible compromised their godly principles as well.

Abraham gave his wife Sarah over to a pagan king, using her beauty and sexuality in exchange for favor and protection.

Jacob deceived his brother into giving up his birthright.

Moses murdered an Egyptian.

Joseph was a tattletale.

David was an adulterer and murdered an innocent man to cover it up.

But God…

But God saved Sarah, telling the pagan king that if he touched her, he'd be a dead man.

But God used Jacob and his two wives to birth the 12 tribes of Israel.

But God used Moses's fear of conviction to drive him deep into the desert to develop him into a man of God.

But God raised up Joseph as a deliverer not only of his own people but of Egypt as well.

But God established David and Solomon in the lineage of Jesus.

Although human beings are far from perfect, God always sees beyond what the human eye can discern. God perceives in our hearts depths and underpinnings that are impossible for us to detect. A deeper look at the story of Esther reveals truth and light, bringing the Lord God and His covenant promise to the forefront of history. As stated earlier, we know from Daniel 4 that the Lord God rules the kingdom of men and gives it to whom He wills.

In the story of Esther, two prominent positions are taken away and reassigned by God's sovereign hand. The Bible states that the king of Persia loved Esther more than all the virgins presented to him, and so he made her queen. Acting on the counsel of Mordecai, she gained one of the highest positions possible—the wife of a king. Mordecai had already attained a position, but God had more ordained for him. Through human agents, God continued to display his faithfulness and justice. He is not a man that He should lie (Numbers 23:19). What He says He will do, He does.

Mordecai had a bitter enemy; his name was Haman. These two men despised each other. Interestingly, a universal bond connected them, one originating hundreds of years before they are even born. In Esther 2:5, read that Mordecai was the son of Jair, son of Shimei, son of Kish, a Benjamite. Saul, Israel's first king, was also the son of a man named Kish, a Benjamite. In Esther 3, Haman was identified as "Haman the Agagite." Agag was the king of Amalek. The Amalekites were bitter enemies of Israel during Saul's reign. Haman was a descendant of King Agag. The crux of this is that Mordecai and Haman were the representatives of two nations—one nation blessed by God through covenant with Him, and the other an enemy of God.

Remember, nothing happens out of nothing. King Saul disobeyed God's instructions to kill the captured King Agag. Instead, he allowed him to live and even seemed to befriend him. For this disobedience (and others) Saul lost his throne.

Generations later, God still had issues to resolve because of Saul's disobedience. As descendants of Saul, Mordecai and Esther were positioned to deal with the wicked root of the Amalekites as represented by Haman. God's sovereign will was being manifest through their conflict.

Esther found so much favor with the king of Persia that, through a series of remarkable events, the king decreed that all of Haman's household be killed. He then gave Esther authority to have thousands more killed by declaring that the Jews had the right to defend themselves from those sent out to slaughter them. She was also given the authority to institute the Jewish feast of

Purim, a feast that is still celebrated today. Haman had sought to destroy the Jews and cast out Mordecai, but instead, the reverse happened. Scripture says that Mordecai grew greater and stronger in the king's palace.

In our present time, it is disturbing to contemplate the fact that nations are still at war and killing each other. As a Christian leader in government, it would be a hard decision to send troops off to war. It's an extremely difficult choice for any leader to command the death of thousands, yet in the Old Testament, it happened over and over. Esther was not afraid to issue the decree. Indeed, she did what she had to do to preserve her heritage.

The debate on war and peace will continue. In the meantime, remember that Esther was elevated to one of the highest positions in government not based on her education or skills, as she had no experience in governmental affairs. It wasn't about what she knew, but whom she knew. Her promotion was based solely on personal relationships. Her honor and respect gave her great authority and much reward. As the wife of a king, she honored her husband and saved a nation.

While observing governmental leaders today, everyone knows how powerful the influence of a close relative can be, especially in making difficult decisions. Governmental leaders need mentors, good friends, and family to support them, pray for them, and give them counsel when asked. You may be one of those who support an official. If so, the counsel you give could very well change a nation.

11

Nehemiah

In Bible days, the life of the king was in constant danger from those who would use his death to advance their own position. That is why the royal cupbearer was such an important position. It was his job to protect the king from poison drink. He did this by drinking the wine before the king drank. If the cupbearer died, well, at least the king was saved. Given his proximity to the king, the cupbearer usually developed intimate access to the king and the influence that went with it (assuming the cupbearer lived long enough). Cupbearers were well known in the palace and at court, and in many instances became king's confidants.

Nehemiah was the cupbearer of King Artaxerxes I, the Persian king whose domain included Jerusalem. When observing Nehemiah's life, we see specific characteristics and attributes that gave him great favor with King Artaxerxes. The Bible does not state how he rose to that prestigious position, but he was positioned to fill an assignment that would bring him to Jerusalem and fulfill God's promise to rebuild the city walls. The Persian empire ruled Jerusalem, and King Artaxerxes had stopped the rebuilding of the city and its walls because of lies warning him of rebellion if the rebuilding was allowed to continue (Ezra 4:7-23 ESV).

The Government and Its People

In Nehemiah 1, Nehemiah was given a report on the condition of Jerusalem. It was not good news. The walls of Jerusalem were broken down and its gates were burned. In response, he humbled himself with prayer and fasting before the Lord. He wept, repented, and prayed for several months until God gave him strength, vision, and hope for the future of the project. With all that God did for him, Nehemiah plotted out a strategy to accomplish a nearly impossible task. It would require great favor and assistance from Artaxerxes—things that Nehemiah was positioned to acquire.

One of the reasons Nehemiah found favor with the Persian king was his sincere loyalty to the well-being of the king. This influence started when the king asked Nehemiah why his face was so sad. In response, Nehemiah first honored Artaxerxes's authority. Nehemiah had proved his faithfulness to the king by keeping him alive, so when the king heard why Nehemiah was sad and asked him what he wanted, Nehemiah was not afraid to tell the king everything.

> In the month of Nisan, in the twentieth year of King Artaxerxes, when wine was before him, I took up the wine and gave it to the king. Now I had not been sad in his presence. And the king said to me, "Why is your face sad, seeing you are not sick? This is nothing but sadness of the heart." Then I was very much afraid. I said to the king, "Let the king live forever! Why should not my face be sad, when the city, the place of my fathers' graves, lies in ruins, and its gates have been destroyed by fire?"
> Then the king said to me, "What are you requesting?" So I prayed to the God of heaven.
>
> Nehemiah 2:1-4 (ESV)

Nehemiah

Nehemiah was specific on what he wanted to rebuild the walls of Jerusalem; he held nothing back. He laid out a plan before the king for what he would need, how long it would take, and how to arrive safely at his destination. He explained all of this in detail to King Artaxerxes. In turn, the king gave him everything he requested.

> *And the king granted me what I asked, for the good hand of my God was upon me.*
>
> Nehemiah 2:8 (ESV)

Nehemiah received a depth of favor that caused Artaxerxes to reverse his own policy and finance the whole building project. How did this happen? Several keys are here to meditate on why Nehemiah received everything he asked.

- Nehemiah was positioned in a high level of government. This position was established by God. As stated earlier, cupbearer positions were one of the closest to the king. Cupbearers became companions and trusted confidants to the king and queen and many other officials in the court. Nehemiah had proved his loyalty and faithfulness.

- Nehemiah was full of the wisdom of God. He depended on God to answer his prayers while recognizing fully where and how those prayers could be answered.

- Nehemiah wasn't afraid to ask the king for assistance with everything he needed.

- Nehemiah was a visionary and a strategist. He researched and acquired all the information he needed to get the task done.

- Nehemiah had courage. He wasn't afraid of executing the plan, or of asking a king to reverse his edict and allow the rebuilding of the walls.

Equipped with authority and supplies, Nehemiah went to Jerusalem to rebuild the walls—completing a task that he was burdened from God to do. He left the Persian palace as a faithful follower, but to rebuild the walls, he had to become a strong, faithful, leader.

According to Nehemiah 3, Nehemiah broke down the project into different sections and manageable sizes. For labor, he was able to mobilize the whole community to get to work. Not just one or two groups were involved. His skill in leadership brought together all types of workers—priests, city officials, temple servants, goldsmiths, and merchants. Even men who lived outside of Jerusalem came and worked—men from Jericho, Tekoa, Gibeon, Mizpah, Zanoah, Beth Hakkerem, Beth Zur, and Keilah.

His authority, leadership, and organizational skills brought the rebuilding of the walls to a completion in 52 days! Although it was not without opposition. The same hostility and resistance that halted the vision years before came back to challenge Nehemiah.

The first opposing force came from those who would be the most threatened by the new governor and the rebuilding of Jerusalem. Sanballat and Tobiah were governors in the region; Sanballat was the governor of Samaria, and Tobiah was the governor of Amman. Both men ridicule and threaten the work.

The first thing Nehemiah did in response to this opposition was to pray. He didn't try to retaliate with physical force; instead, he asked God to vindicate him. When the fight did become real, Nehemiah used the same organizational skills that got the king to approve the project in the first place. He formed a defense mechanism that ensured the building project would be completed while also defending God's people from attack. He used both the spiritual and natural to combat the opposition. He inspired his people to be courageous, but he also gave placed natural weapons in their hands to defend themselves and their families. In so doing, he took his enemies' threat seriously, but never succumbed to fear, relying instead on God's divine protection. The most important thing Nehemiah did, however, was to KEEP WORKING. He was not persuaded in any way to delay the work; it progressed through the most intense opposition.

In addition to the external opposition, resistance also came from within.

> *Now the men and their wives raised a great outcry against their fellow Jews. Some were saying, "We and our sons and daughters are numerous; in order for us to eat and stay alive, we must get grain."*
>
> *Others were saying, "We are mortgaging our fields, our vineyards, and our homes to get grain during the famine."*
>
> *Still others were saying, "We have had to borrow money to pay the king's tax on our fields and vineyards. Although we are of the same flesh and blood as our fellow Jews and though our children are as good as theirs, yet we have to subject our sons and daughters to slavery. Some of our daughters have already been enslaved, but we are powerless, because our fields and our vineyards belong to others."*
>
> Nehemiah 5:1-5

In response to these charges, Nehemiah became angry and confronted the nobles and officials, demanding that they give back to the people their fields and vineyards, and insisting that they stop charging the people interest. He also refused to take what other governors in the past demanded, saying, *"But the earlier governors—those preceding me—placed a heavy burden on the people and took forty shekels of silver from them in addition to food and wine"* (Nehemiah 5:15 NIV).

Clearly what was happening with some of the treatment of his Jewish brothers was not noble or generous. In fact, it was just the opposite. The poor were being exploited by their own. It was illegal and unjust. Nehemiah makes no excuses for the rich but defends the poor in the gates the way a servant of God should do.

> *But the noble make noble plans, and by noble deeds they stand.*
>
> Isaiah 32:8

In the Amplified Bible, we read:

> *The noble, openhearted, and liberal man devises noble things; and he stands for what is noble, openhearted, and generous.*

The poor need a defender, not an excuser. Nowhere in these Scriptures does it say that the poor were not working or willing to work. Everyone was asked to help rebuild; everyone had a stake in the success of the rebuilding. As a man of God, Nehemiah knew that the wealthy Jews were disobeying the law of God. Leviticus reads:

> *If your brother becomes poor and cannot maintain himself with you, you shall support him as though he were a stranger and a sojourner, and he shall live with you. Take no interest from him or profit, but fear your God, that your brother may live beside you. You shall not lend him your money at interest, nor give him your food for profit. "If your brother becomes poor beside you and sells himself to you, you shall not make him serve as a slave."*

Nehemiah

Leviticus 25:35-37, 39 (ESV)

Nehemiah had to correct the situation. He had to set things in order so that everyone would be in agreement. This was an internal situation, but how could the plan and vision proceed and prosper without addressing the fatal flaws within in his own people? The plan would have failed eventually due to the injustice to the poor and the violations of God's word.

Nehemiah led by example as the governor of Judah. He showed a generous spirit when he refused to take benefits available to him. This enabled the people of Judah to trust his leadership and believe his word. He established a unity among the people so that they appeared and stood before him with one heart. As governor, he instituted national reforms with Ezra the priest. The reading of God's word, prayer, and the service of the temple were all brought back at a national level.

By definition a miracle is "an effector extraordinary event in the physical world that surpasses all known human or natural powers and is ascribed to a supernatural cause." Nehemiah's accomplishments were miraculous acts. According to James Boice, this is the order of Nehemiah's acts that were accomplished in less than one year as governor of Judah:

1. Nehemiah secured Artaxerxes's permission to rebuild the walls of the desolated city. He received permission to go rebuild the walls as well as to reverse a previously established policy regarding Jerusalem.

2. Nehemiah developed a plan for constructing the walls.

3. Nehemiah inspired a defeated and dispirited people. This was important because the people had tried to build before and had failed. It was nearly one hundred years of failure. Nehemiah had to lift them into faith.

4. Nehemiah overcame opposition from outside enemies and from inside his own people.

5. Nehemiah completed the reconstruction of the wall.

6. Nehemiah encouraged and assisted in a national revival with Ezra the priest.

7. Nehemiah reorganized and repopulated the city.[27]

These astounding accomplishments were done through faith, persistence, and courage in God. The fact remains, however, that they were also accomplished through the support of the Persian government. We see that the Church can accomplish important things through government. Large building projects can only be completed with the favor and assistance of city and state officials. Nehemiah is an example of how a person can be positioned to equip and lead people in the practical application of ministry.

12

Apostle Paul and Romans

The book of Romans is as deep as it is wide, delving into many themes, including God's role in civil government and how the Christian community should interact with governing authorities. Paul gets right to the heart of the matter in chapter 13.

> *Let every person be subject to the governing authorities. For there is no authority except from God, and those that exist have been instituted by God. Therefore, whoever resists the authorities resists what God has appointed, and those who resist will incur judgment. For rulers are not a terror to good conduct, but to bad. Would you have no fear of the one who is in authority? Then do what is good, and you will receive his approval, for he is God's servant for your good. But if you do wrong, be afraid, for he does not bear the sword in vain. For he is the servant of God, an avenger who carries out God's wrath on the wrongdoer. Therefore, one must be in subjection, not only to avoid God's wrath but also for the sake of conscience. For because of this you also pay taxes, for the authorities are ministers of God, attending to*

this very thing. Pay to all what is owed to them: taxes to whom taxes are owed, revenue to whom revenue is owed, respect to whom respect is owed, honor to whom honor is owed.

Romans 13:1-7 (ESV)

The context of these words is revealing. At the time this book was written, Rome was the absolute ruling power of the known world and Caesar was considered a god. According to N.T. Wright,

The emperor was the *kyrios*, the lord of the world, the one who claimed the allegiance and loyalty of subjects throughout his wide empire. When he came in person to pay a state visit to a colony or province, the word for his royal presence was *parousia*."[28]

At first glance, it appears that Romans 13 is about quiet submission to a pagan ruler, no questions asked, just be still and keep your head down. But further study reveals that the Apostle Paul was really promoting the lordship of Jesus Christ—the true God and ruler of all the earth.

Paul begins the letter to the Romans by stating emphatically that Jesus is the one true God, and that He should be worshiped above all. Some theologians believe that Paul was actually confronting the rule of Caesar by claiming allegiance to Jesus Christ and pointing to His divine authority and headship. In Romans 1:17 Paul writes that he is not ashamed of the gospel of Christ because it is power, the power of God. As Christians, we follow Paul's example in pledging our allegiance to our Lord and Savior Jesus. Indeed, the gospel of Matthew tells us the same.

And Jesus came and said to them, "All authority in heaven and on earth has been given to me.

Matthew 28:18 (ESV)

Because of this authority, Paul boldly states to Roman Christians—citizens of the most powerful nation on earth—that *"there is no authority except from God, and those that exist have been instituted by God"* (Romans 13:1).

There are several points to observe in Romans 13.

In verses 3-4, Paul is saying that Roman rulers functioned as God's servant, bearing God's sword, and that they need not be feared by citizens doing good. And yet, the Roman world was pagan and worshiped several other gods, none of whom were Jesus. Most of the people worshiped Caesar—a mere man in God's eyes but a deity to the masses. How then could these Roman officials be servants of God when they didn't honor God? The answer is that Paul was not referring to specific officials but the authority they carried. Their authority that was from God, and Paul was sending a message both to Roman Christians and to those in authority: All who carry God's authority will have to answer to the One who gave it.

Governmental authority is given by God for the sake of peace and order. The underlying message of Romans 13 was that as long as the governing officials were operating justly, Christians were to obey them. However, if they were asked to denounce their faith, Scripture is clear that they cannot and should not deny the One who saved them, and so they should obey God rather than man.

It wasn't easy living in Rome as a Christian. The Church had to be on its guard at all times. And yet, note the level of governmental engagement to which Paul exhorted the Church. *"Pay to all what is owed to them: taxes to whom taxes are owed, revenue to whom revenue is owed, respect to whom respect is owed, honor to whom honor is owed"* (Romans 13:7). This is a model for engaging the world as active citizens, not hiding away in darkness waiting for the end. Roman Christians were being instructed to be fully present in the place God had ordained them to live.

We find this principle throughout Scripture. Whatever condition the Church finds itself in, it is to obey the Lord and live.

> *Build houses and settle down; plant gardens and eat what they produce. Marry and have sons and daughters; find wives for your sons and give your daughters in marriage, so that they too may have sons and daughters. Increase in number there; do not decrease. Also, seek the peace and prosperity of the city to which I have carried you into exile. Pray to the Lord for it, because if it prospers, you too will prosper.*
>
> Jeremiah 29:5-7 (ESV)

Note the key phrase here: *"seek the prosperity of the city to which I have carried you into exile."* God ties the people's prosperity to that of the culture in which they find themselves.

Paul has similar words for his protégé Timothy.

> *First of all, then, I urge that supplications, prayers, intercessions, and thanksgivings be made for all men, for kings and all who are in high positions, that we may lead a quiet and peaceable life, godly and dignified in every way.*
>
> 1 Timothy 2:1-2 (ESV)

Both Scriptures admonish participation and prayer from God's people for the regions in which they live, calling Christians to quiet, peaceful, productive lives through prayer and obedience.

Of course, this is not always possible. Remember that Paul was speaking to citizens of Rome—not only the most powerful, but the most organized government at that time. Roman Christians lived at a time known as Pax Romana, a period of relative peace and stability achieved by the Roman Empire from 27 BC to 180 AD. Knowing the conditional nature of this peace may have been on Paul's mind when he wrote in chapter 12:

If possible, so far as it depends on you, live peaceably with all.

Romans 12:18

It would not always be like that. Indeed, the same Rome to which Paul urged loyalty would be the Rome that, in the near future, savagely persecuted Christians through ritualized torture as public spectacle. Indeed, the Church continues to suffer persecution and affliction today. This is why the underlying principle is still to pray and obey and do good as much as we possibly can, even to the point of blessing our persecutors.

Bless those who persecute you; bless and do not curse them.

Romans 12:14

The key to Romans 13 is engagement, participating in society, living by the rules and honoring authority. How much more blessings would come on a nation if more Christians became part of the political process and began to enter places of government?

Governmental positions of authority are given by the God we serve and obey. Following the pattern of Scripture, Christians should be positioned in all types and levels of government to rule, to do good, and to influence many.

The Church needs to enter every place of society. Instead of just praying for ungodly leaders to make good and godly decisions, let's pray for the Church to rise up and possess these leadership places in our government. The Church has the things of God: knowledge, mercy, peace, and forgiveness. We are the people who will rule well and bring stability to their nation.

The Government and Its People

Volume II

How the Church Can
Participate in Government

Introduction to Volume II

In Volume 1, we asked why the Church should be involved in government. In answer to that query, we discovered that government involvement is part of a Christian's biblical heritage. Throughout Scripture, we see the Lord's movement and careful occupation upon His people to effect change on the government in every dispensation.

Having answered the first question—*why*—we will now address *how* the Church can participate in government. Simply put, the most predominate way the Church can participate in government is by being present.

Recall roll call in school when the teacher called your name and you raised your hand to show you were there. The opposite of "present" is "absent." A person cannot participate in class if they are absent. They cannot acquire knowledge or participate in the class. Absence is an empty space that needs to be filled.

The problem with empty spaces is two-fold.

It either means that others need to work harder to fill the void that someone else should be filling. Or the space never gets filled at all, and darkness prevails. Like a neglected piece of soil, weeds will grow and choke out the good plants that are trying to grow.

I went by the field belonging to a lazy man, by a

vineyard belonging to a senseless person. There it was, overgrown with thistles, the ground covered with thorns, its stone wall collapsed.

Proverbs 24:30-32 (ISV)

We all know the home of a sluggard. It's the ramshackle house on the corner with trash spewed everywhere. There are broken-down cars in the driveway, overgrown grass in the yard, and children running around with bare feet and dirty faces. Meanwhile the mother sits on the porch with a beer in one hand and a cigarette in the other. She's on the phone calling the police because the last man in the house ransacked the place and stole her rent money.

This is an absence of authority in the extreme—when the person who is called to occupy the space goes AWOL and no one is left in charge.

When the righteous triumph, there is great elation; but when the wicked rise to power, people go into hiding.

Proverbs 28:12

Christians who are present—not absent—can pay attention to governmental issues, ward off the darkness, and keep the weeds from their sphere of influence in our society. Clearly, this is what Jesus meant in this parable:

"You are the salt of the world. But if the salt should lose its taste, how can it be made salty again? It's good for nothing but to be thrown out and trampled on by people."

Matthew 5:13 (ISV)

The Lord sends us out as the salt of the earth, but why salt? What led him to choose that metaphor? Considering its importance, we need an extensive biblical meaning of salt.

Introduction to Volume II

According to Abarim Publications,

> *In the old world, raw salt was highly sought after (our words salary and sale come from the Latin word for salt). Its bottom line is that it stops decay and disintegration; it keeps together what is supposed to be together by arresting the forces that want to tear things apart.*[29]

The website also talks about how salt's applications fall into distinct categories:

1. Salt draws water and blood out of butchered meat, while fungi and bacteria either die or become inactive. Salt also slows down the oxidation of fats, which is what causes meat to go rancid. Salt stops the decay of something dead.

2. Salt disinfects a wound.

3. Salt was used to "disinfect" people who were deemed so infectious to culture at large that they had to be cut away like putrid flesh from a wounded body. The area was to be turned into a "burning waste, unsown and unproductive," that "no grass grows in it" (Deuteronomy 29:22). In the Bible, two clear instances of this deep cleaning are recorded. (See Psalm 107:34, Jeremiah 17:6, Isaiah 34:9, Zephaniah 2:9.)

4. Salt kills impurities similar to fire. "For everyone will be salted with fire" (Mark 9:49).

In the Deuteronomic School, Moshe Weinfeld submits, "razing and burning of a city and its sowing with salt and brimstone seems to have been the conventional punishment for breach of treaty."[30] He goes on to cite the records of several known Assyrian kings who resorted to that practice after such a transgression. But note that salt is not just a symbol of death; it's the symbol of death of that which is rotten. As such, it is a symbol of healing and regeneration of that which was contaminated (2 Kings 2:20-21).

Throughout the ages, entire wars were fought over salt, and note the similarity between our noun חלמ (melah), meaning salt, and the word המחלמ (milhama), meaning battle or war. The latter comes from the root מחל (laham), which either means to wage war or to eat. It's part of the name of Jesus' birthplace: Bethlehem. When Jesus says: "You are the salt of the earth," he doesn't just mean to say what a fine condiment we are.

Salt, therefore, is an instrument of trial and judgment. It is fatal to death, sin, and sinners, and is life to the saved. The lake of fire (ref. Revelation 19:20) is, by implication, similar to a lake of salt. Note that while sin's ultimate destiny is the "depth of the sea," the surface of the Dead Sea—the saltiest body of water on earth—is the lowest point on earth (ref. Micah 7:19).

The meaning of salt has ties to battle as well. If the church is the salt of the earth, occupying a governmental role must be viewed through the lens of waging war, judging, and cleansing with God's Word. When a person decides to participate in government, they become a fiery salt shaker for the kingdom of God, one that will purge and heal every issue it engages.

With a better understanding of Jesus' parable, we begin to see that the Church is salt to civil government, seeking that which can be accomplished on a deeper level. For instance, consider a Christian who runs for a political office. If that person takes hold of their position and responsibility by faith, the salt within them will begin the process of purifying, preserving, and regenerating the governmental functions they are fulfilling. It will now be possible to stop decay, disinfect the wounds, and heal the contamination present in that office.

Of course, not every person is called to the same levels of civil government, but there are specific instructions that are given to the Church as a whole. Romans 13 is an extensive treatise on the Church's role in civil government, describing the Church's role with beauty and order.

> *Let everyone be subject to the governing authorities, for there is no authority except that which God has established. The authorities that exist have been established by God. Consequently, whoever rebels against the authority is rebelling against what God has instituted, and those who do so will bring judgment on themselves. For rulers hold no terror for those who do right, but for those who do wrong. Do you want to be free from fear of the one in authority? Then do what is right and you will be commended. For the one in authority is God's servant for your good. But if you do wrong, be afraid, for rulers do not bear the sword for no reason. They are God's servants, agents of wrath to bring punishment on the wrongdoer. Therefore, it is necessary to submit to the authorities, not only because of possible punishment but also as a matter of conscience.*
>
> *This is also why you pay taxes, for the authorities are God's servants, who give their full time to governing. Give to everyone what you owe them: If you owe taxes, pay taxes; if revenue, then revenue; if respect, then respect; if honor, then honor.*
>
> Romans 13:1-7 (ESV)

Consider Paul's key words: "*The authorities that exist have been established by God.*" They are the foundation for understanding the importance of government. If a person believes in God and His eternal pathways, the understanding that authority exists because of God is the first step to wisdom. However, it begs the question: How can I be more involved?

Obedience to civil authority is important. Our actions are powerful displays of the glory of God, but it goes deeper than that. Honoring a ruler because of their position in government is a witness to the gospel. Paying our taxes is a witness to the gospel. Respecting the rule of law is a witness to the gospel.

Over the years, I have heard many fellow believers say that they just want to serve God. Those who voice this desire typically look to church ministries for fruitful service. And while some find fulfillment there, others are disappointed trying to figure out the call of God on their lives. Yes, serving in church ministries is important. However, civil rulers are also servants of God. They carry power and authority—the ability to change society for the good of all mankind.

In the following chapters, we will explore the diverse ways a Christian can serve the Lord in the world through governing in various institutions and layers of government.

13

Prayer

In December 1944, at the height of World War II, General Patton called upon his chief of staff Colonel Paul D. Hawkins and Chaplain O'Neill of the Third Army. According to Hawkins, this is how Patton called upon the chaplain to pray:

General Patton: Chaplain, I want you to publish a prayer for good weather. I'm tired of these soldiers having to fight mud and floods as well as Germans. See if we can't get God to work on our side.

Chaplain O'Neill: Sir, it's going to take a pretty thick rug for that kind of praying.

General Patton: I don't care if it takes the flying carpet. I want the praying done.

Chaplain O'Neill: Yes, sir. May I say, General, that it usually isn't a customary thing among men of my profession to pray for clear weather to kill fellow men.

General Patton: Chaplain, are you teaching me theology or are you the Chaplain of the Third Army? I want a prayer.

Chaplain O'Neill: Yes, sir.[31]

In the book, *War As I Knew It*, this prayer was distributed to every soldier in the U.S. Third Army:

Almighty God and most merciful Father, we humbly beseech Thee, of Thy great goodness, to restrain these immoderate rains with which we have had to contend. Grant us fair weather for Battle. Graciously hearken to us as soldiers who call upon Thee that, armed with Thy power, we may advance from victory to victory, and crush the oppression and wickedness of our enemies, and establish Thy justice among men and nations. Amen.[32]

The skies cleared within twenty-four hours. A week of perfect weather ensued, allowing the Allies to advance toward the Rhine. Patton was ecstatic and gave Chaplain O'Neill a Bronze Star.

As a young girl, I loved to play chess. While concentrating on every move, trying to figure out the best way to maneuver around the board, I noticed that the first pieces to be maneuvered would be the pawns. They were used to get closer to the king; it was always about taking out the king. In chess, when a person takes out the opponent's highest authority, their side wins. There have been many theories comparing chess to war. In war, there are tactics, strategies, defense, counter attacks, and breakthroughs. Every soldier has a vital role just as every piece on the chess board has a position. In the wrong position, a knight or bishop is powerless; in the right position, a lowly pawn can take out a king. Strategically, a pawn can support a stronger piece to take out the king, or the pawn can go directly and take it out itself. In Christianity, the pawn is the person engaged in spiritual warfare, prayers, and petitions. Often unheralded because their work is unseen, they are indispensable.

Years ago, I was invited to a women's breakfast at a local church in our city. The speaker was a state senator here in my home state of Washington. She had faithfully served our district for many years. One of her statements to those in attendance was this: "If Christians knew the many things that we are called to vote on every day, they would be on their knees crying out to God for wisdom for their elected officials." There are many paths that a person can take to participate in government. But there is one specific instruction given to the Church, and it is asked of every believer, and that is to pray.

> *I urge, then, first of all, that petitions, prayers, intercession and thanksgiving be made for all people—for kings and all those in authority, that we may live peaceful and quiet lives in all godliness and holiness.*

1 Timothy 2:1-2

Those reasons above are simple enough. We are asked to pray for government in order to live peaceful, quiet lives. The opposite of peace is war. So, praying for governmental leaders will push back the warfare.

Of course, God would not tell us to pray if it were not necessary. But this begs the question: Is the future fixed or fluid? What impact do our actions have on the world and the lives around us? The answer, I believe, is in the scriptural examples of future outcomes based on choices made by people. Indeed, the evidence for cause and effect of certain outcomes is abundant. According to Michael Saia in his book, *Why Pray?*:

> The idea of the absolute predestination of all events is not biblical. The notion that the Bible teaches this doctrine is based on false assumptions about certain passages. Because some events were predestined by God, this does not mean every event in history was determined ahead of time. If all choices are fixed, then

there is no free will, love is a sham, and any relationship with God is worthless.

Consider these scriptural examples Saia references:

But if they had stood in My council, then they would have announced My words to My people and would have turned them back from their evil way and from the evil of their deeds.

Jeremiah 23:22 (ESV)

Notice the words, *"If they had…they would…."*

If only you had paid attention to My commandments! Then your well-being would have been like a river, and your righteousness like the waves of the sea.

Isaiah 48:18 (ESV)

Again, notice the words, *"If only you had…then your well-being would have been…."*

The wisdom which none of the rulers of this age has understood; for if they had understood it, they would not have crucified the Lord of glory.

1 Corinthians 2:8 (NAS)

Notice the words, *"If they had understood…they would not…."*

And you, Capernaum, will not be exalted to heaven, will you? You shall descend to Hades; for if the miracles had occurred in Sodom which occurred in you, it would have remained to this day.

Matthew 11:23 (NAS)

Notice the words, *"If the…it would…."*

This last Scripture speaks to more than just the coming of the Lord; it is also about being watchful and alert in prayer for our leaders and rulers in this world.

*But be sure of this, that if the head of the house had
known at what time of the night the thief was coming,
he would have been on the alert and would not have
allowed his house to be broken into.*

Matthew 24:43 (NAS)

Again, notice the cause-and-effect language: *"If the head of the
household had known…he would have been…."*

There are many broken places in government that need to
be restored. So looking back at our instruction, IF WE pray for
authority, THEN WE will live a peaceable life. If we stay watchful
and alert, we are protecting our house, city, and nation from being
broken into.[33]

Let's not forget the most famous Scripture of all,

*If my people, who are called by my name, will humble
themselves and pray and seek my face and turn from
their wicked ways, then I will hear from heaven, and
I will forgive their sin and will heal their land.*

2 Chronicles 7:14

Notice the words, *"If my people…then I will…."*

Another beautiful truth about our relationship with God is the
ability to change God's mind. It's awe-inspiring to realize that we
are heard by our creator and he considers our reasoning and our
opinions when we pray. Consider Moses' interactions with God.

*The Lord said, "I have seen these people and they
are a stiff-necked people…leave me alone so that my
anger may burn against them and that I may destroy
them. Then I will make you into a great nation." But
Moses sought the favor of the Lord, "O Lord, why
should your anger burn against your people, whom
you brought out of Egypt with great power and a*

mighty hand? Why should the Egyptians say, 'It was with evil intent that he brought them out, to kill them in the mountains and to wipe them off the face of the earth'? Turn from your fierce anger; relent and do not bring disaster on your people. Remember your servants Abraham, Isaac and Israel, to whom you swore by your own self: 'I will make your descendants as numerous as the stars in the sky and I will give your descendants all this land I promised them, and it will be their inheritance forever.'"

Exodus 32:9-13

Then the Lord changed his mind and did not bring on his people the disaster he had threatened.

Exodus 32:14

Moses reasoned with the Lord, explaining why destroying His people was a bad idea. In fact, he gave the Lord three specific reasons, showing that his entreaty to God was well thought out. This is not a symbolic story. If we can believe Scripture, Moses changed God's mind.

Consider how Abraham reasoned with the Lord about the destruction of Sodom.

The men turned away and went toward Sodom, but Abraham remained standing before the LORD. Then Abraham approached him and said: "Will you sweep away the righteous with the wicked? What if there are fifty righteous people in the city? Will you really sweep it away and not spare the place for the sake of the fifty righteous people in it? Far be it from you to do such a thing—to kill the righteous with the wicked, treating the righteous and the wicked alike.

Far be it from you! Will not the Judge of all the earth do right?" The LORD said, "If I find fifty righteous people in the city of Sodom, I will spare the whole place for their sake." Then Abraham spoke up again: "Now that I have been so bold as to speak to the Lord, though I am nothing but dust and ashes, what if the number of the righteous is five less than fifty? Will you destroy the whole city for lack of five people?" "If I find forty-five there," he said, "I will not destroy it." Once again he spoke to him, "What if only forty are found there?" He said, "For the sake of forty, I will not do it." Then he said, "May the Lord not be angry, but let me speak. What if only thirty can be found there?" He answered, "I will not do it if I find thirty there." Abraham said, "Now that I have been so bold as to speak to the Lord, what if only twenty can be found there?" He said, "For the sake of twenty, I will not destroy it." Then he said, "May the Lord not be angry, but let me speak just once more. What if only ten can be found there?" He answered, "For the sake of ten, I will not destroy it." When the LORD had finished speaking with Abraham, he left, and Abraham returned home.

Genesis 8:22-33

Abraham was able to get God to change His mind several times. Of course, we'll never know if the Lord could have been talked out of destroying Sodom to save one righteous person. The point is that God and Abraham engaged in dialogue, and God changed His mind.

One more recorded example of a person changing God's mind

is found in Amos 7.

> *This is what the Sovereign LORD showed me: He was preparing swarms of locusts after the king's share had been harvested and just as the late crops were coming up. When they had stripped the land clean, I cried out, "Sovereign LORD, forgive! How can Jacob survive? He is so small!" So the LORD relented. "This will not happen," the LORD said. This is what the Sovereign LORD showed me: The Sovereign LORD was calling for judgment by fire; it dried up the great deep and devoured the land. Then I cried out, "Sovereign LORD, I beg you, stop! How can Jacob survive? He is so small!" So the LORD relented. "This will not happen either," the Sovereign LORD said.*

> Amos 7:1-6

All Amos had to do to change God's mind was to argue that Jacob was small and would not survive if the Lord destroyed the land. It didn't take much reasoning with God. So, was the Lord just looking for someone to ask him to stop? It's hard to tell. What we do know from these examples, however, is that God responds to prayers and petitions, and everything is on the table.

Some people are called to intercession for the government and its officials. This is no easy task. Intercession is deep and takes much time and energy. The prophet Daniel was a governmental intercessor. His actions support the view that the future is not fixed, but instead responds to our involvement.

> *In the first year of Darius son of Xerxes (a Mede by descent), who was made ruler over the Babylonian kingdom in the first year of his reign, I, Daniel, understood from the Scriptures, according to the*

word of the LORD given to Jeremiah the prophet, that
the desolation of Jerusalem would last seventy years.
So I turned to the Lord God and pleaded with him in
prayer and petition, in fasting, and in sackcloth and
ashes. I prayed to the LORD my God and confessed.

Daniel 9:1-4a

Consider the evidence. If the will of the Lord is predetermined, why was Daniel so concerned about praying, fasting, and repenting for his people and his nation? In Daniel 10, Daniel set himself to pray for twenty-one days. Derek Prince, in his book, *Praying for the Government*, gives a fascinating take on Daniel's intercession.

> Daniel set himself to pray for twenty-one days with special earnestness for divine intervention on behalf of his people. At the end of this period, an angel came with a revelation that was the answer to his prayers.
>
> The angel told Daniel: "From the first day that you set your heart to understand and to humble yourself before your God, your words were heard; and I come because of your words." Daniel prayed for twenty-one days, yet his prayer was heard the first day. Why did he have to wait twenty-one days for the answer? In verse 13, the angel went on to give the reason: "But the prince of the kingdom of Persia withstood me twenty-one days; and behold, Michael, one of the chief princes, came to help me." This "prince of the kingdom of Persia" was not a human being. These events did not take place on the human plane. It was an angel who brought the message, and it was an angel who opposed the angelic messenger. Another angel, Michael, came to the assistance of the first angel. This was a spiritual

warfare of angels in the heavenlies. Notice, it was what happened on earth that decided the course of events in heaven. This is a tremendous truth. Nothing happened until Daniel started to pray. It was Daniel's prayers that got the angel through, not the angel that got Daniel through. Daniel got the angel through! If only God's people would see that the issues are settled by us. They are not even settled by the angels. Revelation 12:11 tells us: *"They"*—God's people on earth—*"overcame him"*—Satan—*"by the blood of the Lamb, and by the word of their testimony."* We are the decisive factor in the affairs of the universe. I am not exaggerating one bit. If Daniel had not prayed, things would never have happened in heaven. He had to pray for twenty-one days to get the answer. What delayed the answer? This was not because Daniel did not pray according to the will of God. There was nothing wrong with his prayer. Satan, in the person of the prince of the kingdom of Persia, was the reason for the delay.[34]

The future is not fixed. Everything is negotiable with God. Prayer is the leverage that we possess to change the world in which we live.

How and what we pray is equally important. First of all, a prayer can't be in a void. Being specific as possible increases faith and opens the deep heart. It's a good idea to know the names of the leaders in civil authority. What is the mayor's name? What does he or she stand for? What are the names of the people on the local school board? What kind of decisions are they making for the children in their district? Is the state legislature trying to pass ordinances and laws affecting religious liberties or personal liberties? Knowing what's on the docket and what's being debated in session gives more substance to our prayers and intercession. Praying for wisdom is good, but specific directed prayer is better. In Scripture we see Jesus saying, "What can I do for you?" He asks us to give specific requests. To get started on your prayer journey, here is a website with several guides. These guides are a foundation. Use them, and then personalize your prayers according to what is happening in your own city, region, and state.

When it comes to government, the one thing we are all asked to do is pray. Set aside some time, weekly or bi-weekly, to lift up our governmental officials and the issues concerning our time.[35]

14

Vote

The vote is the most powerful instrument ever devised
by man for breaking down injustice,

Lyndon Baines Johnson

If the statement above was believed and practiced, instead of half the American population voting, every person that could vote would vote. In the 1988 presidential election between George Bush and Michael Dukakis, 91,602,291 American people showed up to vote and 91,050,000 registered voters did not vote in that election. In the 2000 presidential election, after an intense recount process and the decision of the United States Supreme Court in Bush v. Gore, Governor George W. Bush officially won Florida's electoral votes by a margin of only 537 votes out of almost six million cast, and as a result, won the national presidential election.

Did you know that in 1840, women in the United States could not vote, sit on juries, or hold public office? In 1848, at a women's rights convention in Seneca Falls, women for the first time publicly demanded the right to vote. The media made fun of the women and the convention. It's stunning to think how hard women had to fight for the right to vote. In 1865, eight months after the Civil War ended, the government created the Thirteenth Amendment, which outlawed slavery. Then along came the Fourteenth Amendment with the right to citizenship and equal protection of the laws. But this still only applied to males over twenty-one. In came the Fifteenth Amendment that stated the right to vote could not be denied because of race, color, or whether they had been slave. Oops! Only men apply, please!

Because the Fifteen Amendment didn't include women, it caused a rift in the women's suffrage movement. Some women were content that the African-American vote was won first. Others felt it was a sting to both black and white women alike. It took marches, protests, printed articles, and many organized meetings to bring the women's-right-to-vote campaign to the public. There were rifts between family members, especially between husbands and wives, and fathers and daughters. There was also an anti-suffragist movement led by women. These women argued that families would be destroyed because women would rebel against their husbands if they had the right to vote. There were major industries that fought hard against women voting. Cloth manufactures employed huge numbers of women and were afraid that they would use their political power to fight for higher wages. Liquor manufacturers were against women voting because many women supported the temperance movement.

Then in 1878, twelve years after the first convention, a senator from California introduced an amendment for women's suffrage that became known as the "Susan B. Anthony Amendment." It didn't pass, and that amendment would be brought up before Congress every session for 42 years! Imagine for a moment being a woman living during these years. At that time, the media mocked women's suffrage leaders through political cartoons. In one cartoon, a woman voter was depicted as abandoning crying babies in the arms of her husband to go out and vote. These women were seen as rebellious troublemakers that wanted to ruin the fabric of society. The husbands of suffragists didn't have it easy, either. They were called henpecked and accused of tagging after the girls. The husbands were ostracized and told to go home and do the dishes. There were many heated augments between the husbands of suffragists and anti-suffragists. In 1917, a Quaker woman named Alice Paul even went to prison for picketing in front of the White House.

It finally came to a volatile head two years later when the Senate voted in favor of the Nineteenth Amendment, giving women the right to vote. In order for the bill to become law, however, three-quarters of the states had to ratify the amendment. The women of the suffrage movement had to convince thirty-six lawmakers to vote in favor of the amendment. It literally got down to one state—Tennessee—where it flew through the Senate but stalled in the House of Representatives. The governor called a special session to vote on the amendment. The fight for the vote in Tennessee became known as the "War of the Roses." Lawmakers in favor wore yellow; those opposed wore red. There was a deadlock vote 48-48 and weeks of intense debate and lobbying. The suffragists wondered when their fifty-two-year battle would finally come to fruition.

On the day of the vote, Harry Burns–one of the youngest lawmakers in the House—entered the capitol building wearing a red rose. Everyone turned to Burns. With his red rose on his lapel, he spoke out loudly in favor of the amendment and reversed his opposing vote. Shock filled the room. The anti-suffragists were furious, but the suffragists cheered and rejoiced with all their hearts. It was such an intense battle that Harry fled to the attic of the state capitol and hid until the angry crowds dispersed. Some say he even crept onto a third-floor ledge to escape an angry mob of anti-suffragist lawmakers threatening to rough him up. He said later that the one reason he changed his vote at the last minute was that his mother asked him to.

One of the founding leaders of the suffrage movement, Carrie Chapman Catt, is quoted as saying,

> To get the word *male* in effect out of the Constitution cost the women of the country fifty-two years of pauseless campaigning.... During that time, they were forced to conduct fifty-six campaigns of referenda to male voters; 480 campaigns to get legislatures to submit suffrage amendments to voters; forty-seven campaigns to get state constitutional conventions to write woman suffrage into state constitutions; 277 campaigns to get state party conventions to include woman suffrage planks; thirty campaigns to get presidential party conventions to adopt woman suffrage planks in party platforms; and nineteen campaigns with nineteen successive Congresses.
>
> Millions of dollars were raised, mainly in small sums, and expended with economic care. Hundreds of women gave the accumulated possibilities of an entire lifetime, thousands gave years of their lives, hundreds of thousands gave constant interest and such aid as they could. It was a continuous, seemingly endless chain of activity. Young suffragists who helped forge the last links of that chain were not born when it began. Old suffragists who forged the first links were dead when it ended.[36]

Everything we have as rights and privileges has been fought

and paid for by someone. The right to vote came through the perseverance of many women from Christian and other religious circles. To be effective, these people had to come out of their religious comfort zones and join a political movement. They had to choose to speak up for what they knew was right. This brought criticism and hardship. In their hearts, these women knew they were paving the way for justice. And yet, true and unending justice comes from one place—the heart of God the Father. The fact that God-fearing women took up the fight, leaving their church pews and the comfort of their places in society, has given me as a woman the right to vote according to my conscience, my values, and my morals.

Voting is a right that millions of Americans take for granted every election cycle. To this day, half the population doesn't participate in the vote. Why not?

Why Don't We Vote?

1. Many people lack an appreciation of the power of the vote. They need to understand, from an early age, the importance of voting. In the United States, voting is a privilege and a right. It's a responsibility and stewardship for the citizens. Voting needs to be held in high regard, first in the family and then in the schools. Parents can teach their children at a young age that regardless of the outcome, voting is an obligation that must be done in the same way we pay our taxes.

2. Voting is hard because the issues that we are called upon to vote on are often complex. It takes time to study the issues and understand what the candidates believe and stand for.

3. People don't care about things that don't affect them personally. If a person doesn't own a home or a business, the tax laws don't concern them. Yet hundreds of decisions are made every

day in state capitols that affect a person's life in diverse ways.

4. Voting doesn't seem to make a difference, so many people are indifferent. But in reality, voting does make a difference. Recently, here in Washington state, a House seat was overturned by the opposite party, giving them control of the House by a single seat margin. In some elections, a seat is won or lost by a single vote. When power shifts to another party, the leadership of every committee changes to the new party. This means that every bill that the leading party wants to pass will be considered first because the majority rules. This also means that the many bills by the minority party will not be considered. Bills eventually become laws, and once a law is enacted, it is difficult to reverse. So a single vote can have an impact for years.

What Does Our Vote Represent and Where Is It Counted?

1. The president and vice president, governors and lieutenant governors.
2. The Congress and the Senate to represent our state in Washington, D.C.
3. The state representative and state senator to represent and work on behalf of our local districts.
4. The school boards.
5. City council members.
6. County council members.
7. Tax bills.
8. Laws concerning drugs and health care—for instance, the legalization of marijuana.
9. Social laws involving marriage, parental rights, and children's rights.

When an issue is able to make it to a ballot, the voter decides which way it will go. In some instances, less than half of registered voters participate in their local elections. In the state of Washington, only 27 percent voted in the fall of 2017. That's twenty-seven out of one hundred voters.

The way to resolve this problem is messaging. First, make sure your family and friends are registered to vote. If they are not, begin the conversation as to the important role they can assume once they become a voter. If you are a parent, don't just tell, but show. Take your children with you to the ballot box. Teach them respect for the process. Young children can learn through picture books and older children can be taught basic fundamentals of an issue (explain it in simple terms). We don't need a degree in political science to vote. There are many groups that have voter guides that can answer questions about a certain candidate or issue that is on the ballot. The media has changed. Now a person can turn to social media outlets and find out both sides of an issue on the ballot and decide which best fits their values.

Voting gives the Church and other groups an opportunity to voice their concerns and fears. Voting is the power that creates change. It's the way that Christians can participate in government.

15

<u>Citizen Lobbyist</u>

On November 12, 1997, in Schenectady, New York, an eighteen-month-old tabby cat named Buster was outside doing what curious cats do—running, hiding, playing with other cats, and wondering when he'd get to eat again. On this particular night, a sixteen-year-old boy named Chester Williamson observed Buster, grabbed him, doused kerosene all over his body, and lit Buster on fire with a cigarette. Buster was found by a neighbor under a car and immediately rushed to the vet. He was so badly burned, he had to be identified by his large nose and number of toes. Buster lingered for three weeks but finally succumbed to his injuries. This led to a new law called Buster's Law. In 1999, Governor Pataki signed Buster's Law, also called the Felony Cruelty to Animals Law.[37]

> In the case of Buster's Law, Nancy Bonesteel took her shocking experience of what happened to her cat and made a difference in the laws concerning animal cruelty. Buster's Law brought attention to another aspect of animal cruelty. Aside from the injuries to the pets themselves, there is evidence that violence against animals can be a precursor to violence against

humans. Activists need look no further than Buster's tormentor, Williamson, to support their argument. In 2003 and 2005, Williamson was sent to prison on stolen property and burglary convictions, sentenced to up to three years in both cases. Then, on Sept. 28, 2007, just a few blocks from where he attacked Buster, Williamson, then 26, lured a 15-year-old into Vale Cemetery under the pretext of looking for her sister and attempted to rape her. Officers searching the cemetery came upon Williamson and the girl, breaking up the attack. Williamson is now serving in the state prison.[38]

What is a Citizen Lobbyist?

A citizen lobbyist is a person who tries to get legislators to introduce or vote for measures favorable and against measures unfavorable to an interest that he or she represents. What drives citizens to become lobbyists? Usually, it is passion for an issue that resonates with their personal or professional lives. This passion often comes because of traumatic personal experiences or deeply held beliefs about justice and personal freedoms.

In the last twenty years, tragedy has met several parents, and some of them have used what happened to their children to start foundations and change laws. In September 2006, 19-year-old Brodie Panlock ended her life after enduring ongoing humiliating and intimidating bullying by her co-workers at a café in Hawthorn, Victoria, Australia. Brodie was insulted and ridiculed, teased about her looks, held down while fish sauce was poured over her, teased about a failed suicide attempt, and had rat poison put in her bag while being taunted about being unable to kill herself. They regularly insulted her by calling her fat, stupid, ugly, and a whore.

The tragedy of Brodie's death was compounded by the fact that none of those responsible for bullying Brodie were charged with a serious criminal offense under the Crimes Act 1958. Instead, each offender was convicted and fined under provisions of the Occupational Health and Safety Act. Brodie's death was a tragic reminder of the serious consequences that bullying can have on victims, their families and the community and illustrated that there were obvious limitations in the law and conduct involving serious bullying and should be subject to criminal sanctions. Because of public outrage and aggressive citizen lobbying, Brodie's Law commenced in June 2011 and made serious bullying a crime punishable by up to 10 years in jail.

In the United States, there have been other laws enacted named after victims. Megan's Law is named after seven-year-old Megan Kanka, who was raped and killed by a known child molester who had moved across the street from the family without their knowledge. In the wake of that tragedy, the Kankas sought to have local communities warned about sex offenders in the area. All states in the U.S. now have some form of Megan's Law.

Passion for an issue doesn't need to stem from adversity. There are thousands of issues that concerned citizens can work on to make a change. The first question to ask is, "What issue brings out an emotional response when there is a discussion or debate?" Anger and fear are good indicators, and channeling those emotions through advocacy is productive. The first step in advocating and lobbying for an issue is thorough and in-depth knowledge of the topic. If all a person knows about a topic is some strange headline from social media, how can that person answer in-depth questions on the topic? Studying all aspects of the topic is important to becoming an effective advocate. With every legislative issue, there are people who are for it and against it. It is important to know these things:

- Who is in leadership on both sides of the issue?
- Why are some for advancing the issue and why are some against advancing the issue?
- What are the history and current status of the legislation concerning the issue?
- What are the barriers to passing the legislation?

Simply screaming, "Our rights are being taken away, and this county is going to hell," is not going to advance a cause with the people who have the authority to change the situation.

After fully understanding the issue and preparing for every possible question, there are several ways to bring attention to the topic. One productive way is to start a petition. According to Care2petitions,

> A petition, put simply, is a list of names and signatures compiled together to show support for a cause. By demonstrating public support, petitions give clout to an issue that could otherwise go overlooked by government or business. Whether you are looking to change a law or a behavior—or just raise awareness for an issue—petitions are an easy and inexpensive way to get the word out.[39]

Here are some questions to ask:

- Is your case petition ready?
- What do you need to know to make your petition ready?
- Which groups, businesses, and influencers support your cause?
- Do you have a clear target?
- Can this petition open a dialogue?[40]

- One person can do a variety of things, but there is strength in numbers. That is why it's a great idea to consider joining a nonprofit organization that has similar values as your own on issues and laws that need to be implemented or changed. Partnering with an organized group helps in several ways. The most obvious one is finances. In most cases, it takes money to get attention. That is why nonprofits are getting more proficient at marketing and promoting their cause. Many organizations offer educational tools, workshops, training sessions, and conferences on fundraising. Partnering with organizations keeps the momentum and personal passion going while encouraging people to work together on the same issue, building deep and lasting friendships.

Social media is a powerful tool, but it can also be destructive if used poorly. Participating in a group discussion with comments is helpful.

Here are some important keys to remember when posting on social media:

- Stay on topic with the issue that is being discussed.
- Be polite, but firm. No personal insults, profanity, or name calling.
- Use social media in moderation, especially when it comes to political issues.

Hammering out tweets hourly and spouting out all day on Facebook about a topic will drive people away simply because they will tire of hearing the same thing. Updates and information are good; obsessive complaining and murmuring is not good. Negativity is never conducive to winning over your peers. It's also a good idea to create dedicated Facebook pages and other social media accounts for each topic at hand. This way, you will be able to post on your specific topic to a targeted audience and avoid annoying your friends and family.

The most vital participation a citizen lobbyist can make is contact their elected officials at every level of government. Although some people may feel intimidated about doing so, we should understand that our public officials work for the citizens. Still, there is a protocol to such contact. Most important is to not waste the official's time. That is why you should know the topic from beginning to end and be specific about what you want the official to do. Next, make sure you are reaching the right person. Is your issue a city, state, or federal issue? It could be a combination, so educate yourself in order to communicate to the right people. Find out who are your state and U.S. legislators. It's easy to check. Just log on to your state government website, type in your zip code, and in most states the website will direct you right to the correct legislator in your district.

Investigation is easier these days because every branch of government has a website. For instance, here in Washington State, the website is leg.wa.gov. From there, a person can get information on bills, committees, scheduled hearings, and floor sessions. There are separate pages within the website specifically for the House and Senate Republicans and Democrats. Further, each legislator has a personal page, and that page shows what bills they are sponsoring. When the state legislature is in session, there will be 4,000 to 5,000 bills for them to consider. It's simply impossible for them to understand every issue. In many instances, they are instructed by their caucus on how to vote.

In order to be an effective citizen lobbyist, a person has to think from the perspective of a legislator. According to the Family

Policy Institute of Washington State, "To influence the behavior of a legislator, there needs to be knowledge of what motivates their decisions."[41]

Fundamentally, there are three types of legislators. The first is the legislator that agrees with the issue and is participating on the same team. The second legislator is equally against the issue and on the opposite side. Then there is the third legislator that sits squarely in the middle. It is this third legislator that determines what issues get voted on and is the deciding vote on controversial bills. He or she is the person who needs to be persuaded on the issues.

There are four distinct ways to educate a legislator:

1. Facts
2. Studies
3. Budgets
4. Policy arguments

When approaching a legislator, it is important to understand their thinking and motivation on key issues. The number one deciding factor with many votes is, "How will it impact their reelection?" The next question is, "Do they have a conviction about the issue?" If they do—one way or another—it will be difficult to make a persuasive argument. If there is no conviction about the issue, the legislator will consider your arguments.

Now, to a legislator, thinking about an issue is not the same thought process as a vote. A voter looks at an issue from deeply held values. A legislator—especially those in the middle—will ponder several things before casting a vote:

Interest groups

Will the vote affect the interest groups that are giving them money?

Chairmanships

Will the vote jeopardize future leadership positions within the party?

Peer groups

What kind of consequences will come from peers and associations?

Impact on position in caucus

Will the vote upset the party line and caucus?

Higher office

Will the vote impact future chances for higher office?

A citizen lobbyist needs to identify and get to know the legislators who can be persuaded—those in the middle. Build a respectful relationship with your legislator, not a combative one. The middle legislator needs to become an ally. Work on discovering their focus and goals for their term. Getting involved with issues that are bipartisan is a good head start in relationship building. The goal is to build bridges, not burn them.

Here are three ways to reach out to legislators.

1. Phone calls

Every legislator has a phone number listed on the state capitol website. Their phone will usually be answered by their legislative assistant or staffer. Still, these are human beings, so don't be a robot reading off a template. Their offices get those types of phone calls every day, so droning on and on will do little to advance your cause. Instead, explain in your own words your opinions and feelings about the issue. Stay on topic and to the point. Two good times to call are at the beginning of the legislative session and right before the vote.

2. Email

Every legislator has an email that can be taken directly from the State Capitol website. Be specific with emails. When addressing a government official, in person or in print, use the proper salutation. This signals to your representative or senator that you respect their position, and they will be more likely to take you seriously.

The proper salutation for a U.S. senator is "Dear Senator <name>."

The proper salutation for a U.S. representative is "Dear Mr./Mrs./Ms. <name>."

Of course, there is no legal requirement to use a particular salutation. You're free to call your senator or representative whatever you like. However, you will gain favor and be taken more seriously if you respect the office of the person you're contacting.

It is also important to write with a friendly yet professional tone. Your email doesn't have to be a work of art but it needs to be free of spelling and grammar mistakes. Access the plethora of editorial software available; much of it is free (such as Grammarly). Finally, if you're asking the official for a particular change, be firm and state your position clearly.

You may include personal details but try to keep them relevant to the topic at hand.

Keep written correspondence short. Don't write more than a few paragraphs if you want your reader to stay with you. Make sure you say what you need to say. Condense any anecdotes as much as possible. Try to keep it under 500 words, and be polite and courteous.

3. Visit in person

Visiting your legislators can be daunting, but most of them realize they work for their constituents, and so they will listen to your concerns. Make an appointment in advance. Prepare for your meeting with a written outline. Greet them with grace, especially if they are from the other side of the aisle. Find some issue they have voted on or sponsored where there is an agreement between both of you, and thank them for it. Be courteous, smile, and get to the topic. If you are nervous, you might forget an important point, so bring a note card and keep it close. Stay away from generalities such as, "We need better education!" or, "The roads are a mess." Bring the issue to your personal experience. How will the issue affect you, your family, your community? Explain in detail the consequences and the benefits of their vote. The legislators need to be reminded that their votes affect thousands of people exactly like the one sitting across from them.

And again, do not waste their time. Choose your words carefully, and give them time to process your information. They are busy people; respect that.

In conclusion, be alert and stay abreast of the information affecting your issue. Join groups, use social media, sign petitions, march at rallies, and visit your legislator face to face. You can make a huge impact for today and change your world for tomorrow.

16

The Neighborhood

It was 6:00 p.m. and Amy was on her evening run when a neighbor that she never met rushed up to her and said, "Amy? Are you Amy? Please get in the car. There's an issue with your son." Without hesitation, she jumped in the car and allowed the man to drive her to her home. Upon arrival, there were police cars and an ambulance parked at her home.

"Is my son okay?" she cried out. "What happened? Where are our other boys?"

Here is the rest of the story in her words.

> After his third "I don't know…your husband just asked me to find you" response, I tried to silence my chatter. When we finally pulled up to our house, I saw my husband, Brandon, on his knees, head on the grass, with a small, shirtless body lying next to him: my Jack. "Is he gone?" I squeaked, inching my way in beside Jack amidst a sea of unfamiliar faces. My heart was in my throat, and I was shaking.
>
> Brandon lifted his head and brought his hands to his face. He couldn't speak. He looked ghost-white. Horrified. Broken.

A stranger, a petite blond with warm eyes and a calming demeanor, stepped up to me. "I didn't think I could save him," she said, "but I did CPR, and I think he's okay."

I later learned that her name was Barbie. She was a registered nurse, and though I'd never seen her before, she lived across the street from us.

Her words hung in the air.

Didn't think she could save him? He had actually been gone? Not breathing? She had brought him back to life?

I reached for her hand and squeezed it, then scooped Jack into my arms and collapsed on the grass, speechless with the terror of what might have been.

What could I say to the woman who had literally saved my son's life, the woman who hadn't thought she could save my baby but had tried—and done it? Her will, her skill, and her breath had brought him back to us.[42] This is one story among countless others of how the people living right next to us have the potential to help in time of crisis. Think about it. Our neighbors share our most intimate space, our everyday natural life. What are those spaces? They are our homes, roads, shopping malls, restaurants, schools—everything a person needs to live life is shared with our neighbors. Yet according to Brian Bethune in his article "The End of Neighbors" "More than 30 percent of Canadians now say they feel disconnected from their neighbors, while half of Americans admit they don't know the names of theirs, and a recent poll of 2000 Britons found a third couldn't pick out their neighbors out of a police lineup."[43]

It's worse that not knowing our neighbors, however. In recent times, we have stopped *caring* for our neighbors. Yes, social media has brought a social revolution, but neighborhood involvement has been declining for decades. Neighbors stopped talking to each other long before video games and Facebook. One reason for this is economics. Fifty years ago, families lived on one spouse's income while the other spouse—usually the mother—stayed at home. This brought a neighborhood filled with family members watching over each other's children and properties. Now, most neighborhoods are completely vacant during the day with a few hours in the later afternoon and evening occupied by latchkey kids playing video games, watching TV, or on social media. Compounding the problem is the fact that when we are home, we are usually recovering from the day, and by then it's difficult to get out of our personal space and reach out to a stranger, even when that stranger lives one hundred feet from your front door or shares a backyard fence.

The tragedy in this social evolution is that the neighborhood remains the most available evangelistic field for most Christians. Most of us will not be able to go to Africa, but we can reach out to the single mom or the lonely elderly man across the street, as scarce as they are becoming. According to Scripture, Christians are to love their neighbor as themselves. In Luke 10, the question posed to Jesus was, "Who is my neighbor?" His answer became the parable of the good Samaritan.

> In reply Jesus said: "A man was going down from Jerusalem to Jericho, when he was attacked by robbers. They stripped him of his clothes, beat him, and went away, leaving him half dead. A priest happened to be going down the same road, and when he saw the man, he passed by on the other side. So too, a Levite,

when he came to the place and saw him, passed by on the other side. But a Samaritan, as he traveled, came where the man was; and when he saw him, he took pity on him. He went to him and bandaged his wounds, pouring on oil and wine. Then he put the man on his own donkey, brought him to an inn, and took care of him. The next day he took out two denarii and gave them to the innkeeper. 'Look after him,' he said, 'and when I return, I will reimburse you for any extra expense you may have.'

"Which of these three do you think was a neighbor to the man who fell into the hands of robbers?"

The expert in the law replied, "The one who had mercy on him."

Jesus told him, "Go and do likewise."

Luke 10:30-37

According to the teaching of Christ, this word "neighbor" is any other man irrespective of race or religion with whom we live or whom we chance to meet (which idea is clearly brought out in the parable).[44]

Jesus used this parable to dig out from the Jewish community an ugly root of racism, but he also dealt with people's tendencies to look the other way and refused to get involved. This parable teaches us just the opposite. When a need becomes evident, the Christian community is expected to fill that need and not ignore it.

What good is it, my brothers and sisters, if someone claims to have faith but has no deeds? Can such faith save them? Suppose a brother or a sister is without clothes and daily food. If one of you says to them, "Go in peace; keep warm and well fed," but does nothing about their physical needs, what good is it? In the same way, faith by itself, if it is not accompanied by action, is dead.

James 2:14-17

How does the Church participate in government by being a good neighbor? Well, the neighborhood consists of homeowners and taxpayers, and each group has certain rights and authority. As such, a neighborhood is a form of government. Taking responsibility to bless and help the neighborhood is releasing God's light in darkness.

Indeed, there here are many ways to engage people in the local neighborhood. It's important to build relationships in the neighborhood so when there is a crisis, the neighbors will know whom they can ask for help, prayer, or guidance. In most instances, personal salvation comes first from the seed, then the shoot, then the final harvest. The ideas below are ways to start planting seeds and sharing the love of God.

Here are some great ideas:

- Get to know your neighbors. If you can't name more than a neighbor or two, it's time to introduce yourself. Even if you've lived in your home for a while, this first introduction doesn't need to be awkward or a big production. Simply smile and say, "Hey, I've been meaning to introduce myself…"
- Hang out on your porch or in your front yard. It's hard to get to know your neighbors if you don't ever see them. Just by being out in front of your house you can give off a welcoming vibe that encourages interaction. If I am out in front, especially with the kids, every neighbor who walks by, even those I don't know, still smiles and says hello.

- Create a block directory. If you don't yet know your neighbors, this is the perfect way to get started. It doesn't need to be fancy. Just drop off a sign-up sheet in everyone's mailbox, and, once they return it to you, you can email the final version to everyone.
- Be respectful of your neighbors. Don't be that guy they all talk about. Clean up after your dog, and keep it leashed when out walking. Be aware of any disturbing noise levels that you are creating. Maintain your property, and respect property boundaries.
- Organize a block party. I didn't learn most of my neighbors' names until we had our first block party. After that one party, it seemed there was a lot more interaction on our block. This idea does involve a little work, but if you share the coordinating duties with other neighbors and keep it simple (at least that first year), this is an easy way to get to know your neighbors.
- Build a little free library. As a book lover and a community builder, I've always loved the idea of the little free library. And we're lucky to have two within a couple of blocks of our house (one a residence, one a business). Each little free library is registered online, so you can even see if there already is one near you.
- Build a community garden. This is a time-tested way to promote community interaction in your neighborhood as well as share in a bounty of fresh veggies. Check out the American Community Gardening Association's steps for getting started.
- Host a backyard movie night. Treat the neighborhood to your favorite movie.

- Create a formalized tool-sharing program. Sure, you can just ask Joe next door if you can borrow his drill, but consider establishing a more formal tool-sharing program to get everyone involved. I love this idea because tools are one of those things that you generally only use once in a while, so why not share them when they're not in use? Local Tools is an online lending library management system that can get you started. Or check out Peerby or Streetbank to see if your neighbors are already participating.

- Welcome new families. You can bring a traditional baked good, but I also love the idea of welcoming newcomers by sharing your favorite local restaurants and businesses, perhaps with a stack of your favorite take-out menus wrapped up in ribbon.

- Establish a neighborhood watch program. These programs can be one of the most effective deterrents to neighborhood crime. Check out the National Crime Prevention Council's guide to getting started.

- Celebrate Neighbor Day in April. Since 2010, Good Magazine has sponsored Neighbor Day on the last Saturday of April by providing tools and suggestions to encourage good neighboring. You can check the website to get neighborly inspiration from all over the globe.

- Host a regular monthly gathering, same time, no RSVP needed. Years ago, I read in Sunset Magazine (unfortunately, the article does not appear to be archived online) about a woman who hosted a monthly soup social at her house. The idea was simple: She provided the soup, and neighbors would bring a baguette or drink to share, and their own bowl. And this was key: She held it at the same time every month and no RSVP was necessary. A regular gathering that requires no commitment and little forethought makes for an easygoing gathering.

- Start a neighborhood book club. In my last neighborhood, we had a block book club. When you only have to walk two houses over, it is a lot easier to be able to participate. Or if that feels like too much commitment (and when your kids are young, reading an entire book each month can feel like an unattainable goal), consider something slightly different, such as an "articles club."

- Shovel your neighbor's sidewalk when it snows, especially if it is difficult for them. If you neighbors are older or perhaps just going through a hard time with a new baby or sickness, spend a few extra minutes to clear their sidewalk too. This is no small gesture. In Denver, homeowners can actually be ticketed if their sidewalks aren't clear 24 hours after it snows, even if they are out of town. Plus, you never know who will return the favor.

- Support your neighborhood schools. There is a reason the most successful schools are the ones where parents are actively engaged. Good schools have successful, if informal, partnerships between the administration, the parents, and the community-at-large. Even if you don't have kids at the school, it's important to remember that the local school is also a member of the community and can greatly impact the neighborhood, positively or negatively. Our neighborhood businesses frequently host fundraisers to benefit the local schools. If you can attend an event, you're helping the school as well as getting to know your neighbors at a fun community event.

The Neighborhood

- Address concerns or issues directly with your neighbor. Don't let a problem fester and escalate. And don't immediately call to report a problem to the city without first trying to work it out with your neighbor directly.
- Host a porch party. This is something I've always wanted to do! I love hanging out on my front porch, and a porch party feels like an easy way to socialize with your neighbors without the work of a "real" party.
- Shop locally if you live near a business district. You will not only see and interact with your neighbors at the local businesses and along the way, but you will also get to know your other neighbors, the local business owners and employees.
- Support our youngest entrepreneurs by buying the neighbor kids' lemonade. I once read somewhere you should always buy whatever kids are selling on card tables in their front yards. I think it goes back to the "it takes a village" concept where you're helping to encourage the initiative and resourcefulness of the young. Plus, just think back to when you were a kid and you were so excited to have a lemonade stand. You made all of the lemonade and spent an hour working on your sign, and then you sat and waited and waited. And when that first customer finally showed up, it didn't matter that you only made fifty cents; you were so excited. Be that person for the neighborhood kids.
- Treat your neighbors to a front-yard concert. Music has always been something that brings people together. Still, this one's a little tricky and depends on the neighborhood. Many would welcome a guitarist strumming on his front steps but perhaps not a full band. You have to know your

neighborhood and, of course, be aware and respectful of noise levels. Check out Boulder's Mapleton PorchFest for inspiration.

- Share your skills. Are you tech savvy? Perhaps you can sew or like to tinker with cars. Your neighbors would love for you to share these skills with them, either by teaching them or just helping on a one-time basis. Skill-sharing banks are popping up in neighborhoods across the country.

- Talk to other parents at the park. The neighborhood park is where I get the best scoop! If you have kids, the neighborhood playground can offer a wealth of info: which schools parents like and why, where the best activities for kids are, which new restaurants are coming to the neighborhood. Exchanging neighborhood info at the park is a time-honored tradition among parents, but so often today everyone is on their smart phone. And I admit, I've been that mom. But I've also learned to make play dates and gather neighborhood intel.

- Coordinate a neighborhood yard sale. Garage sale, tag sale, yard sale…whatever name you call it, this is a good way to clear out your home's clutter and help your neighbors do the same.

- Start a networking group. Like the old nursery song goes, you just never know "who are the people in your neighborhood, the people who you meet each day." One of them just might be the perfect person for you to connect with professionally. Who knows? Your next position or client could be as close as the guy who lives four houses down. Meet up at a neighborhood coffee shop, and publicize it on their community board to cast a wider net in the neighborhood.

- Let your neighbors know when you will be out of town, and ask them to contact you or the police if anything is suspicious. You don't need a formalized neighborhood watch program to keep the neighborhood safe. My next-door neighbor had a break-in stopped by a helpful neighbor who knew she was traveling. If you ask your neighbors, they will likely ask you in turn, which helps to keep the neighborhood safe for everyone.

- Welcome new little ones to the neighborhood. When I was growing up, every time one of the families had a new baby, the neighbors would decorate the families' front porch with pink or blue ribbons. It was a small gesture, but a way of simultaneously announcing to everyone the baby's birth and welcoming the baby into our community.

- Share small neighborhood gifts at holiday times. It's rare that anyone gets anything fun in the mail these days. Why not surprise your neighbor with a holiday treat? Keep it simple: baked goods, seasoned popcorn, or even a bottle of wine will be welcomed by most.

- Drive like your kids live here, because they do! I have become one of those people who yells, "Slow down!" whenever a car speeds down our street, which means I've become my parents. But, I get it now that I have kids. We all like to live in vibrant, bustling neighborhoods, but this means people, especially kids, need to feel safe when walking or biking around.

- Connect online to connect offline. Websites like Next Door have created whole new online neighborhoods, but it's important to remember to not use these sites in place of actually getting to know our neighbors in real life. So, go ahead and create that neighborhood Facebook group page. But, be sure to use it to encourage offline interaction, too.[45]

17

City Government

September 11, 2001

The attack on the twin towers in New York City was an attack of unprecedented magnitude. This quote by then mayor Rudy Giuliani captures the feeling well.

And as we are walking toward the scene, which was only two blocks away, looking up, all of a sudden I see a man throwing himself out of the 101st, 102nd floor. And I would say that experience, I describe it as like a switch. It just changed all my emotions. I went from sort of a feeling that I'm walking through an emergency that I can handle, that we've had before. We have a game plan. We know everybody has their role. When I saw that, I just exclaimed to people around me, "This is much worse than anything we've ever faced before. It's off the charts. We're just going to have to make up our response, we don't have a plan for this."

And that scene, of the man throwing himself off the building, I probably relive more than any other. When I go back to September 11th and think about it—lots of memories, but the one persistent and most difficult one is watching that man throw himself from the 101st, 102nd floor. Because it probably shocked me, and I just watched the whole thing. I just stopped and watched the whole thing.[46] With the president out of sight for most of that day, Giuliani became the voice of America. Every time he spoke, millions of people felt a little better. His words were full of grief and iron, inspiring New York to inspire the nation.

Tomorrow New York is going to be here. And we're going to rebuild, and we're going to be stronger than we were before…I want the people of New York to be an example to the rest of the country, and the rest of the world, that terrorism can't stop us.[47] New York City is the largest city in the United States. Being the mayor of that city is a weighty position with massive accountability. But on September 11, even the mayor had no idea what it would entail to be a civil servant. A huge need appeared that day, requiring him to become more than a mayor. He became a light and a hero for millions.

In the city of Seattle, there is a plan to build heroin injection sites for the addicts. In response, Jon Nehring, the mayor of Marysville, Washington, (a community north of Seattle), and his son Nate Nehring (who has a seat in the Snohomish County council) brought concerns to the county council regarding injection sites in their community. The Snohomish County council unanimously voted against having heroin injection sites brought into their region. Not only did they ban injection sites, but the local government is currently taking proactive steps to prevent an infestation of homeless addicts. They are launching the new North County Law Enforcement-Embedded Social Worker Team, as well as a new county chronic nuisance ordinance. There will be two social workers from the county and three law enforcement officers going into encampments where the homeless and drug-addicted dwell. The goal is to offer assistance and connect them with treatment, job training, and services that will sustain them until they are fully capable of living a healthy and stable life. If they refuse, under the new law, the lifestyle of an addict will not be tolerated. Many of these addicts commit property crimes and abuse the local community. If the addict does not want to change, they will be removed from the city. This is tough love, yet in this case, the local government is taking responsibility for their community. (As a side note, both Jon Nehring and his son, Nate, are Christians.)

Getting involved in local city government may not always be that dramatic, but people in every city need strong leaders and visionaries to help guide and build the city. Cities need leaders who have integrity, leaders who are fearless and bold in decision making, leaders who are full of faith. Cities need leaders who will protect and oversee the citizens with care. And yet, at deeper level, Scripture says this about Christians who live in cities.

> *When the righteous prosper, the city rejoices; when the wicked perish, there are shouts of joy. Through the blessing of the upright a city is exalted, but by the mouth of the wicked it is destroyed.*
>
> Proverbs 11:10-11

Christian leadership is vital to any city.

> *Unless the Lord watches over the city, the guards stand watch in vain.*
>
> Psalm 127:1

How does the Lord watch over the city? He watches over the city through His servants, including His civil servants. And to what end? Well, at the end of the age, there will be a separation of sheep and goat nations. Is it possible there could be the same for cities? Cities are a creation of God, so much so that at the end of the age, the glorious bride comes down as a beautiful city. These earthy cities could be training for ruling and leading in the ages to come. Christian men and women could completely transform their cities from corruption and poverty by faith in God and by the wisdom of the Holy Spirit.

The local city government has several departments and many services, all necessary to keeping a city functioning at peak performance. In fact, it's breathtaking to take in how a local city works.

Here is a basic list of city departments and definition of a few of their roles:

Mayor

The mayor occupies the highest elective office in the municipal government and is expected to provide the leadership necessary to keep the city moving in the proper direction. Effective mayors see themselves not only as leaders staking out policy positions but also as facilitators of effective teamwork.

As a mayor, you have a special set of long-term responsibilities not shared by many others. You are supposed to be a community leader and a political leader. Yet most of the trials and tribulations you will face during your term of office will deal with city housekeeping. These day-to-day activities are of immediate concern to most residents, and sometimes solving the little problems are the most fun.

Ceremonial role: The mayor's participation in local ceremonial events is a never-ending responsibility. On a daily basis, the mayor is expected to cut ribbons at ceremonies to open new businesses, break ground for construction of new city facilities, and regularly appear at fairs, parades, and other community celebrations. The mayor also issues proclamations for a variety of purposes. As featured speaker before professional clubs, school assemblies, and neighborhood groups, the mayor can expect to be interviewed, photographed, and otherwise placed on extensive public display by the media.

Intergovernmental relations: The city does not operate in a vacuum. Cities must work within a complex intergovernmental system. City officials keep in contact and cooperate with your federal, state, county, and school officials. Mayors take the lead in representing their local government to those from outside the community who are interested in joint ventures–including other local governments, regional organizations, and federal and state government representatives. In this area, mayors promote a favorable image of their local government and pursue resources that will benefit the community.

Public relations: Mayors inform the public, the media, and staff about issues affecting the community. This role is critical in building public support and facilitating effective decision-making by the council.

Working with residents: Mayors listen to complainants, inform the residents, and encourage participation.

The City Council

In general, it is the council's role to adopt policies for the city and it is the mayor's role to administer or carry out those policies. The council, being legislative, has the power to enact laws and policies, consistent with state law, usually through the enactment of ordinances and resolutions. The council also has specific authority to:

- Enact a city budget.
- Define the powers, functions, and duties of city officers and

employees.

- Fix the compensation of officers and employees.
- Establish the working conditions of officers and employees.
- Maintain retirement and pension systems.
- Impose fines and penalties for violation of city ordinances.
- Enter into contracts.
- Regulate the acquisition, sale, ownership, and other disposition of real property.
- Provide governmental, recreational, educational, cultural, and social services.
- Impose taxes, if not prohibited by state law.
- Cause the city to own and operate utilities.
- Approve claims against the city.
- Grant franchises for the use of public ways.
- License, for the purpose of revenue and regulation, most any type of business.

In addition, the council is authorized to enact rules governing its procedures, including for public meetings and hearings.[48]

Police Department

Police officers are trained and sworn to uphold law and order. A normal duty shift might include transporting a drunk driver to a detoxification facility, intervening in a domestic assault, citing underage drinkers, apprehending a shoplifter, handling a traffic accident, investigating burglaries, and executing search warrants. Each call requires completion of forms and reports. Occasionally, an officer will be summoned to testify in court about the incident and circumstances of the arrest. Along with traditional duties, police officers today engage in many proactive initiatives. They get out of their cars, walk around, and interact with families and business owners in their assigned neighborhoods. An effort is made to get acquainted on a first-name basis with leaders of schools, organizations, and churches. Examples of proactive outreach include helping to organize a neighborhood watch, giving presentations to schools, and speaking to residents about their concerns at a neighborhood association meeting. Building trust with diverse communities and working collaboratively to address social issues, such as gang violence, is an especially important function of the police.[49] The Bible has some interesting Scriptures about police officers, besides the duties already listed. Romans 12:4 says, *"For the one in authority is God's servant for your good. But if you do wrong, be afraid, for rulers do not bear the sword for no reason. They are God's servants, agents of wrath to bring punishment on the wrongdoer."* One translation calls rulers policemen. Notice what the Lord calls these rulers with swords: His servants. They are His servants for our good. How much more good if these servants were the bearers of Christ's light?

Here are some other departments and their roles taken from the City of Marysville, Washington, website:

Fire Department

Besides putting out fires, the fire department educates the public about these workshops and services:

- Smoke alarms and carbon dioxide detectors
- Preventing falls for older adults
- Blood pressure checks
- Child passenger safety
- Bike helmet program
- Address signs
- CPR classes

Courts

Court judges have jurisdiction to preside over traffic infractions, misdemeanors, gross misdemeanors, and codes.

Community Development

Community development is a one-stop shop for developers, citizens, and property owners to obtain information, permits, online payment of residential permits, and assistance on all aspects of land use and land development. It enhances customer service by providing easy access to staff and planning and building documents while streamlining the permit process. It provides consistency and predictability of land development from the initial planning stages all the way to final approval.

Finance

The finance department provides financial services for the city. It provides staff and citizens with services in accounting, taxes, treasury, budgeting, capital investment, purchasing, and contracting.

Parks and Recreation

The parks, culture and recreation department's focus is to enhance the quality of life by providing beautiful parks, open spaces, and exceptional recreational and athletic programs. The department has a long history of providing the public with exceptional parks and services for children, families, and individuals by providing a safe and fun environment for everyone to experience.

The parks, culture and recreation department coordinates several festivals and events each year. A wide variety of recreation and athletics classes, camps, leagues, trips, and tours are available year-round to cater to the active and creative spirit in everyone.

Public Works

From traffic signals to wastewater treatment plants, the public works department provides leadership in preparing, building, and maintaining the infrastructure that provides for our community's needs today and for the generations of tomorrow.

Regular operations include:

- Maintaining and constructing sewer, water lines, and storm drain systems
- Maintaining water quality
- Managing surface water
- Maintaining the wastewater treatment plant
- Maintaining traffic signals and street signs
- Striping, sweeping, and maintaining streets for all weather conditions
- Managing engineering/capital projects
- Maintaining the solid waste, recycling, and yard debris program
- Providing mapping services
- Maintaining city vehicles and facilities
- Purchasing and distributing supplies for department operations
- Providing administrative support for the department as well as customer service

The people who work for the city are called public servants for a good reason. For the most part, public servants will not become rich from their position. Unlike the corrupt early years, city officials have a passion and love for their city. The first thing a person can do to get involved in city government is to attend a local city council meeting, ask questions and get to know the leaders of the community. In a city, a person can touch others in a variety of ways. The easiest way a person can participate in city government is by shopping and purchasing locally. The city sales tax goes into the city coffers. Invest where you live. It's a great first start.

18

The Schools

Children will spend half of their lives in school starting around the age of six and ending around the age of twenty-one. Where a child lives and how much money the family makes will determine the quality of instruction he or she will receive. Parents have options, but those options revolve around finances and time. There are several ways a child can be educated. The local public school, a private institution, charter schools, homeschool, and tutoring. Most families place their children in public school. Public school requires very little parental involvement other than the child bringing home notices and the parent/teacher conferences. In some instances, the public school teaches things that are contrary to the parents' values and religious beliefs. In these cases, the parents have rightful authority to challenge the school.

Here are some examples where public schools have crossed the line.

Mackenzie Frazier, a sixth-grader at Somerset Academy, a public charter school in Las Vegas, Nevada, was told that she could not include a Bible verse in a class assignment titled "All About Me." And organization called First Liberty sent a demand letter to school officials informing them that the law protects the expression of faith by students in class assignments. Two days later, the school responded with a formal apology and allowed Mackenzie to resubmit her assignment including her expression of faith.

First Liberty is one of several organizations dedicated to "*defending and protecting our country's most cherished and profound freedom: religious liberty.*"[50] *Here are more stories from their archives.*

> A teacher at Park Lakes Elementary School in Ft. Lauderdale, FL, ordered Giovanni Rubeo to stop reading his Bible during the free reading time, saying, "Put it on my desk." The teacher then left a voicemail for Giovanni's father, telling him that "those books" were not allowed in her classroom. First Liberty Institute sent a letter to the school, demanding an official apology and restoration of students' rights. The school rescinded the threats, ensuring that Giovanni and his peers may now read their Bibles during free time.
>
> First Liberty Institute successfully protected the religious freedom rights of Audrey Jarvis, a college student at Sonoma State University in California who was told by a supervisor to remove a cross necklace while she was working at a student orientation fair. First Liberty helped Audrey file a request for religious accommodation with the university. After an investigation by the university, the school's president issued Audrey a formal apology.
>
> Audrey's story demonstrates that religious liberty can be preserved when those who experience the violation of their rights courageously take a stand. Audrey's

case made headlines across the country, bringing attention to the growing attacks on religious freedom in America's schools and universities.

Angela Hildenbrand, the valedictorian of her class and a model student at Medina Valley High School near San Antonio, Texas, planned to pray during her graduation speech. However, a federal judge banned prayer from the school's graduation ceremony and threatened incarceration for anyone who disobeyed his order. First Liberty Institute filed an emergency motion for intervention and request for relief on Angela's behalf at the U.S. Court of Appeals for the Fifth Circuit. The Fifth Circuit overturned the lower court's ruling and protected Angela's right to pray at her graduation ceremony.

The federal district court's order violated Angela's constitutional rights to religious liberty and free speech. The government cannot censor the religious speech of its citizens, including public school students. The First Amendment of the U.S. Constitution guarantees the rights of free speech and free exercise of religion, and the U.S. Supreme Court affirmed that students do not "shed their constitutional rights to freedom of speech or expression at the schoolhouse gate" (Tinker v. Des Moines Independent Community School District, 1969).[51] Consider this line from the previous paragraph: "Students do not shed their constitutional rights to freedom of speech or expression at the schoolhouse gate." This is a profound sentence. Christians need to be thankful for the right to voice their belief in Christ. In order to keep this right strong, Christians can step up to the plate and participate in their children's school. Public schools are government-sponsored institutions funded by the taxpayer, administered by school boards and school superintendents. Once a child enters under that "public gate," they come under authority. That authority has the power to instill values and beliefs contrary to the parent or guardian over that child. Because of strong civil authority, parents and guardians are often manipulated or intimated by teachers, principals, and administrators. These gatekeepers hold great power, but they do not have the highest authority over children. Children belong to their parents, not the government. Parents need to recognize the battle in which we are engaged.

Nehemiah faced a similar battle when he undertook to build a wall and restore the gates of Jerusalem. Nehemiah 4:17-18 reads, *"Those who carried burdens were loaded in such a way that each labored on the work with one hand and held his weapon with the other. And each of the builders had his sword strapped to his side while he built."* Obviously, Nehemiah wasn't looking for a fight—the objective was to finish building the wall—but he recognized that he had to be prepared for battle.

Parents are engaged in building families. In so doing, they are required to engage and uplift their families, but also to defend and protect them. Good parenting means being proactive in the children's lives. It is vital that parents operate from both offensive and defensive positions when it comes to their families.

> *Teach them to your children, talking about them when you sit at home and when you walk along the road, when you lie down and when you get up.*
>
> Deuteronomy 11:19

> *Arise, cry out in the night, as the watches of the night begin; pour out your heart like water in the presence*

*of the Lord. Lift up your hands to him for the lives of
your children.*

Lamentations 2:19

These Scriptures (and there are many more on this topic) are
instructing parents to pray for their children and teach them the
Word of God daily. This is the offensive tactic. The defensive tactic
is going on the battlefield and protecting the children from the
corrupt influences of our day.

In recent years, government-run schools have tried to
indoctrinate children on a variety of subjects. A recent development
is the attempt to remove the pronouns "he" and "she" from the
English vocabulary. The argument is that calling a boy a boy and
a girl a girl is somehow discriminatory. This is how far the public-
school rabbit hole will go without accountability and oversight.
There are 48 million students in the United States, 90 percent of
whom attend public schools.

Consider the power that school boards wield:

- Taxing authority

- Employing the superintendent

- Developing and adopting policies, curriculum, and budget

- Overseeing facilities issues

- Adopting collective bargaining agreements

To get in front of the issue and to ensure the best possible
outcomes for the next generation, it is vital that Christians
participate in the public-school forum at a much deeper and
more focused level. School board members are elected, so run for
office. Becoming a school board member will keep the Christian

community abreast of what types of curriculum, events, and worldviews are promoted by public schools and handed down to our children.

Here are some other ways parents and guardians can participate in government-run schools.

PTA

The Parent Teacher Association is a national organization geared toward building strong relationships between parents, teachers, and administrators. This relationship is for the sole purpose of strengthening and advocating for students.

The PTA provides the following benefits:

- Regular updates on school activities and policies
- Access to teachers and administrators at your child's school
- Access to parents of other children at the school
- A forum to discuss concerns and problems at school
- Access to resources on parenting, education, and more from the National PTA
- Appreciation from teachers for all your help
- Education about school policies, state funding, and other issues concerning your school

If the problem needs attention from the state or national government, any local, district or state PTA can bring the issue to the attention of the national PTA.

The PTA is extensive organization and a great place to get rooted in your local community for the children. Parents and guardians don't need a college degree to be involved and can still be a strong pillar for the children and youth in their sphere of influence.

Here is an extensive list of the things the PTA does for the school districts:

Learning: PTA supports a rich, well-rounded curriculum for all students—not just reading, writing, and arithmetic, and not just textbooks, rote learning, and bubble tests. All children deserve literature, history, the arts, hands-on math and science, project-based learning, physical education, sports opportunities, and more.

The arts: PTA supports the arts for all students. That means diving in and making things, or performing, or writing. It's all about creative expression, not just observing someone else's work.

Children's health: Many PTAs act in supporting roles to ensure children's health needs are met. Health issues impact a child's entire life, including his or her ability to focus, study, and learn. Imagine trying to absorb knowledge while suffering with a toothache.

Beginning with prenatal care and "well-baby care," parents should make sure that their children have routine medical and dental checkups so that problems are averted or discovered and treated as early as possible. Check for vision and hearing problems. It's hard to learn if you can't hear the teacher, or if you can't see the board.

Mental health: PTAs and other organizations offer parental education, especially in areas of social/emotional health such as anxiety, depression, substance abuse, and bullying.

Parent education: PTAs all over the country offer talks and workshops on health and safety, learning, special education, parenting, and other topics. Most are free; many are open to everyone. Did you know that the SCCOE presents over 200 free workshops each school year? Colleges and universities, hospitals and clinics, foundations, churches, and other agencies and nonprofits all over the country also offer great talks and workshops (some free).[52]

Booster Clubs

My parents divorced when I was ten years old. At the beginning of the divorce, me and my siblings were required to live with our father instead of our mother. My father was not a Christian and didn't understand the purpose of marriage and family, but he was a hardcore disciplinarian who loved sports. At ten years old, he signed me up for a girls' softball league in the city. That was the probably the greatest accomplishment of parenting he did for me. I was a natural. I learned quickly how to play and became a champion ball player. In the process, I learned discipline and the importance of being part of a team. I learned what it felt like to win and what it felt like to lose miserably. My dad never missed a game and kept me in sports until the middle of my high school years. His directing me into sports saved me from the substance abuse and lawlessness that often comes from hours of inactivity and boredom.

Parents and guardians need to understand the importance of attending their children's events and strive to play an active role. Joining a booster club or starting one for their school sports teams can be a way to become more involved, fostering accountability with the coaches and teachers who are involved in the school team sports.

Here is a brief description of what a booster club does (according to Steele Canyon High School's club):

- [They] raise money to defer costs of athletics, athletic team support, and the Athletic Department of SCHS.
- [They] strive to improve positive communication between school coaches, the school administration, student athletes, and parents.
- [They] provide rewarding opportunities for parents to

participate in their student's athletic experience.

- [They] raise money through memberships, fundraising events, merchandise sales, concession sales, corporate sponsorships, and generous donations.
- [They] help organize and empower Team Liaisons to make certain every team is represented and fellow parents receive necessary information. [53]

As good as children's sports programs can be, they can also inflict harm. I've met many people whose children have be hurt by coaches and team leaders through bullying, personal favoritism, and other injustices that can happen through sports. If Christian parents get involved, acting as the light and salt in school sports, their children will experience a much healthier and more rewarding experience, with less of the trauma that comes from a prideful, unjust spirit.

Here are some other ways a parent or guardian can get involved in their children's schools:

- Chaperon field trips or dances. If your child thinks it's just too embarrassing to have you on the dance floor, sell soft drinks down the hall from the dance.
- Serve on the school committees or advisory councils as a parent representative.
- Help on projects, such as editing the school newsletter.
- Help in your child's class, in the school library, in the cafeteria, or in the school office.
- Make food for a school event.
- Tutor students in areas such as reading, math, English, Spanish, computer skills, or other subjects.
- Work in a parent resource center or help start one. In these school centers, parents may gather informally, borrow

materials on parenting and children's schoolwork, and get information about community service.[54]

The public school environment is a minefield of positive and negative impacts. Socially, children are placed in an environment that does not reflect adult life. Considering the fact that children spend the majority of their time in the hands of public educators who may or may not hold the same values as the parent, it is imperative that parents keep a keen eye on daily activities that go on in these institutions.

19

State and National Government

Here in the United States of America, our government is operated by three branches—the judicial, the legislative, and the executive. These correspond to the offices we commonly know as the Supreme Court, the Congress, and the presidency. These three branches were designed by our founding fathers to act as a balance for each other, ensuring that no single branch gained too much power. To the framers of the Constitution, the number three must have seemed right—fewer branches and power could be consolidated; more branches and power would be hopelessly fragmented.

The number three is significant in many ways, chief among them the fact that we serve a triune God composed of the Father, Son, and Holy Spirit. Here are some more remarkable three-facts:

- Our planet is in the third orbit from the sun.
- There is the law of the thirds in painting and photography.
- There are three primary colors.
- In theater, literature, and music, there are often three main parts.
- We see in three dimensions—length, width and depth.
- There are three means of heat transfer: radiation,

conduction, and convection.

- There are three classifications of rock: igneous, metamorphic (or pyroclastic), and sedimentary.
- The triple point of water is in three phases: solid, liquid and vapor.
- There are three laws of motion and three laws of thermodynamics.
- Time is past, present, and future.

But the most significant way the number three is shown is that Jesus Christ our Lord was crucified, buried, and rose from the grave on the third day.

Three is a powerful number that obviously came from the mind of God. Did our founding fathers think about its origin when they formed our government? Possibly. So, where did they get the idea of three branches of government?

Our constitution was written by men who followed the writings of Charles Secondat, Baron de Montesquieu. James Madison relied heavily upon Montesquieu's theory of the separation of powers when drafting the Constitution. Montesquieu argued that the best way to secure liberty and prevent a government from becoming corrupted was to divide the powers of government. But where did Montesquieu receive this initial truth of three branches? He got his ideas from a more famous philosopher, Aristotle. In Book IV Chapter 13 of his Politics, it reads,

Having thus gained an appropriate basis of discussion we will proceed to speak of the points which follow next in order. All constitutions have three elements, concerning which the good lawgiver has to regard what is expedient for each constitution. When they are well-ordered, the constitution is well-ordered, and as they differ from one another, constitutions differ. There is (1) one element which deliberates about public affairs; secondly (2) that concerned with the magistracies—the questions being, what they should be over what they should exercise authority, and what should be the mode of electing to them; and thirdly (3) that which has judicial power.[55]

So, following the trail, where did Aristotle receive his information? Whatever writings he was studying, there is no question that the three branches of government came directly from the heart and mind of God. In Isaiah 33:22, we read, *"For the LORD is our judge, the LORD is our lawgiver, the LORD is our king; it is he who will save us."*

Amazing isn't it? There it is—the three branches of government. Consider another passage, Isaiah 9:6-7:

> *For to us a child is born, to us a son is given, and the government will be on his shoulders. And he will be called Wonderful Counselor, Mighty God, Everlasting Father, Prince of Peace. Of the greatness of his government and peace, there will be no end. He will reign on David's throne and over his kingdom, establishing and upholding it with justice and righteousness from that time on and forever.*

Are there three branches of government in heaven? Well, there is the Father, Son, and Holy Spirit. The United States government is not perfect, but it definitely follows the pattern from Scripture. So, in our present time, it's workable.

The United States consists of federal government and state government. Government leaders vote on everything that involves our daily life. They vote on taxes, healthcare, transportation, marriage, distribution of goods, education and so much more. On the state level, the legislature will have 4 to 5 thousand bills to consider in each session. The responsibility is enormous.

These two lists show governmental offices that are given by the voting public through elections and the other offices are given by appointment.

Executive Branch—Carries Out Laws:

- President
- Vice president
- Cabinet—nominated by the president and must be approved by the Senate with a least fifty-one votes.

Legislative Branch—Makes Laws:

Congress is divided into two houses, the Senate and the House of Representatives.

- Senate—one hundred elected senators total, two senators per state.
- House of Representatives—435 elected representatives total, representatives based on each state's population.

Judicial Branch- Evaluates Laws

- Supreme court—nine justices nominated by the president and approved by the Senate with at least fifty-one votes.
- Federal courts

State governments have the same three branches of government:

- Executive branch—governor
- Legislative branch—the Senate and House of Representatives
- Judicial branch—supreme court, superior court, tax court

These offices carry significant political weight. If a person aspires to lead in these federal or state offices, he or she must start at the community level.

- Establish a position in the local community as a mayor or city council member.
- Be involved in local elections, volunteer with local

campaigns, and stay current on all the political hot topics in your state.

- Show up for rallies and parades.
- Volunteer at voting booths.
- Get to know the leaders in the political party that hold the same views.
- Get party support, and make friends and allies before deciding on running for office.

In addition to these steps, consider becoming a precinct committee officer (PCO). A PCO helps win city and state elections in a variety of ways. The most important is educating the people in the local district. A PCO builds up the community, shares information, and supports campaigns. They are a vital link to the party they serve.

Education is an important qualification for these higher offices. Almost all congresspeople have a bachelor's degree and many have master's degrees and law degrees. College is not a prerequisite to obtaining political office, but in actuality, the more educated a person is, the better equipped that person will be to serve the people and defend themselves against critics. Online education has made it easier to attain the degrees and move up the ranks to achieve political aspirations.

If the Christian community begins to take hold of the importance of these positions, Christian families can change a community, a city, a state, and our nation. How do we do this? By bringing the political fire to the family first. Engage your children to think about becoming a Supreme Court judge, a senator, or a state treasurer.

From an early age, young people should think about changing the world through government. Becoming an intern is a great first step and has the potential to open doors for future careers. There are thousands of internships in government that can be filled. Many powerful people in government today started out as interns. Interns help with administration, running errands, writing, making phone calls, etc. They also help with research on issues that are up for vote or things that are needed for congressional hearings.

An appreciation for these things needs to be instilled at a very young age. This can be done through family field trips to the state capitol, the White House, and the other places that show the strength of the government. It can also be fun to watch national elections with your family. One of the sweetest memories I will always treasure is the night of the 2016 national election. It was about 3:00 p.m., and I was wanting to watch the election, but according to the media, the election was already over before it began. So, I thought maybe I would skip watching. Then I heard someone turning a key in my front door. My sons are grown and out of the house, but they still have keys. It was my son, Nathanael.

"Hey, what are you doing here?" I asked.

"Aren't you watching the election?" he said.

"No, not yet," I said.

"Well, let's get it on," he said.

"OK, have you had dinner yet?" (Of course, the mom thing kicks in.)

"No. Whatcha got?"

"I can make tacos." (His favorite.)

"YEAH! Let's do it."

So, I began cooking, and he turned on the television.

"I'm texting Jordan to see if he wants to join us," he said about my oldest son.

"Go for it," I said.

"Hey, Jordan wants to know if the tacos are chicken or beef."

"Chicken," I said.

"Are you making rice?"

"Of course I'm making rice."

"He'll be right over."

Jordan came within the hour. Within the next hour, Andrew, the youngest of the three, came over, too. The four of us sat and watched the 2016 election unfold. Nathanael had the remote and kept changing the channels back and forth to watch the different pundits' opinions. Watching how a United States president becomes elected was one of the greatest shows on Earth. The cable news shows made it more suspenseful by not calling the states too soon for fear of making a mistake. We watched the electoral map change from state to state. The energy that was pulsating through me was also going through my sons. We were all on the edge of our seats. My house was filled with awe observing the process, and once again I was given the opportunity to lead my home by answering questions, making comments on their observations, and bonding with my children on an adult level. It was electrifying. Why? Because I have been talking to my children about politics since they were in grade school. The seeds were planted very early.

Mark 4:27-28 reads:

> *This is what the kingdom of God is like. A man scatters seed on the ground. Night and day, whether he sleeps or gets up, the seed sprouts and grows, though he does not know how. All by itself the soil produces grain—first the stalk, then the head, then the full kernel in the head. As soon as the grain is ripe, he puts the sickle to it, because the harvest has come.*

Plant your seeds early to become a public official on the state and national level. Prepare the ground not only for this generation, but for the next one ahead. The Church will reap a harvest of governmental leaders the world has yet to see.

20

International

On May 7, 2017, eighty-three girls were kidnapped from a school in Nigeria by a group of militants called Boko Haram. The name means "western education is forbidden," and they are at war with the West and Christianity. The new leader of this militant group has vowed to bomb churches and kill off Christians in Nigeria.

However, attacks on Christians are not limited to Nigeria. According to the ministry Open Doors, North Korea has been No. 1 on the World Watch List—as the most dangerous country in the world for Christians—for 17 consecutive years. An estimated 80,000–130,000 political prisoners are kept in North Korea's prison camps. Prisoners in the camps are often "tortured and killed on account of their religious affiliation, with officials instructed 'to wipe out the seed of [Christian] reactionaries,'" and "in one account, guards killed a prisoner's newborn baby by feeding it to guard dogs." Further, routine public executions are carried out in front of both children and adults. These displays of cruelty are designed to subdue the prison population.[56]

Colombia, South America, is severely affected by corruption, with the main agents of persecution being leaders of criminal groups such as drug cartels and dissident guerrilla groups. Indigenous leaders also persecute Christians under suspicion of trying to impose their worldview for territorial advantage. Violent Christian persecution is commonplace in this South American country, both at the hands of criminal and indigenous groups. Guerrilla groups force Christians to pay a "protection tax"—which amounts to insurance against assault or murder. They issue death threats to Christians involved in evangelism, fearing that believers will continue to stand in opposition to the reign of terror these groups use to maintain power.

The fact is, there are many Christians all over the world being persecuted for their faith. The Open Doors ministry helps the Christian community with information on ways to help our brothers and sisters in these nations. One way to help is by rising up in governmental positions. The more governmental authority, the stronger the voice. Becoming a diplomat on the governmental scene is a powerful way to combat the persecutions. The next generation of ambassadors will need a strong, passionate vision for the whole world. They will need to be disciplined from an early age and pointed in the right directions to attain these important roles.

According to Diplomacy 101, a U.S. diplomat's mission is to carry out the foreign policy of the United States. This is done in various ways.

Here is a list of what they do:

- Our diplomats support Americans living or traveling internationally for positive events (such as registering a birth of a child) and in times of stress (such as assisting a jailed American citizen or helping to evacuate Americans from danger.)
- They ensure a level playing field for American businesses

overseas.

- They support joint counterterrorism cooperation and criminal investigations.
- They decide who has a legitimate reason to travel to the United States and issue visas accordingly.
- They work to ensure the safety and security of international flights to the United States.
- They fight pandemics and deliver humanitarian aid to those in need.
- They assist governments to respond better to their citizens' needs, making countries more stable and secure.
- They link emerging leaders in government and civil society to American counterparts to foster relationship building and collaboration.

Ambassadors are the chief officers under the United States president at embassies. Under the ambassador, five types of foreign service officers work together as a team.

- Economic (or "econ") officers work with foreign governments to secure internet freedom, fund scientific advances, protect the environment, or negotiate new trade laws.
- Management officers are action-oriented "go-to" leaders responsible for all embassy, consulate, or diplomatic mission operations from real estate to people to budget.
- Political officers keep the ambassador up-to-date on political events and changes occurring in the country.
- Public diplomacy officers build mutual understanding and support for U.S. policies by reaching directly to publics in foreign countries working with traditional and social media; websites; educational, cultural, and sports programs; and

all manner of people-to-people exchange.

Consular officers' primary job is assisting and protecting American citizens abroad. If you lose your passport, find yourself in trouble with the law, or want to get married to a foreigner overseas, you'll need the help of this officer. Consular officers also issue visas to non-U.S. citizens who wish to travel, work, study, or live in the United States.[57] There are positions in government that can be attained, but they take years of planning and work. These positions are called diplomats. A person does not become a diplomat immediately out of college. John Christopher Steven, the Benghazi ambassador who served Libya, served only three and a half months before he was killed by militants in 2012. Before attaining that post, Stevens had this experience:

- He earned a B.A. in history in 1982 at the University of California, Berkeley.
- From 1983 to 1985, he taught English as a Peace Corps volunteer in Morocco.
- He graduated with a J.D. from the University of California, Hastings College of the Law in 1989.
- He received an M.S. degree from the National War College in 2010.
- Stevens was an international trade lawyer based in Washington, D.C.
- He was admitted as an active member of the State Bar of California on January 26, 1990.
- He went on inactive status on August 1, 1991 and remained an inactive member for the remainder of his career.

Stevens joined the United States Foreign Service in 1991. His early overseas assignments included these:

- Deputy principal officer and political section chief in

Jerusalem
- Political officer in Damascus
- Consular/political officer in Cairo and consular/economic officer in Riyadh.
- In Washington, Stevens served as these:
- Director of the Office of Multilateral Nuclear and Security Affairs
- Pearson Fellow with the Senate foreign relations committee and Senator Richard Luga
- Special assistant to the under secretary for political affairs
- Iran desk officer and staff assistant in the Bureau of Near Eastern Affairs.

He had served in Libya twice previously: as the deputy chief of mission (from 2007 to 2009) and as special representative to the National Transitional Council (from March 2011 to November 2011) during the Libyan revolution. He arrived in Tripoli in May 2012 as the U.S. ambassador to Libya.

Stevens spoke English, French, and some Arabic.[58] The goal of a Christian is to be an ambassador for Jesus Christ.

We are therefore Christ's ambassadors, as though God were making his appeal through us.

2 Corinthians 5:20

If more Christians prepared themselves to become political diplomats and officers for their countries, then many glorious gates would open to these nations. The authority that is vested in these posts allows for the Christians in these positions to call upon the Lord for salvation, protection, and for guidance and strategies all over the world to root out the evil forces. As stated above, these officers are up-to-date on all political events and changes that occur in the country they are assigned.

I, like millions of other Christians, do not know when the Lord is returning the second time. It may be awhile. Therefore, Christians need to understand what it would take to train their children and grandchildren to aspire for these political posts. Becoming an ambassador or a diplomat is a long and arduous process. In addition, these positions are usually political appointments. The people who receive these appointments have been involved in political circles and have family, friends, and associates to turn to to receive these positions. Christians need to grab hold of this vision as a way of changing the world. An ambassador to any nation is a gate of authority and could do much good for the kingdom, especially if that ambassador has a prophetic/evangelistic mantel. We need to train and raise up the next generation of international prophets.

Prepare early to become a world changer. Instill the desire in your children and grandchildren to become involved in international affairs. Visit a local diplomat, ask questions, find out exactly what the starting points would be to go from desire to the actual execution. The church is still the answer to all the world's deepest problems.

21

<u>Conclusion</u>

In making the case for why the Church should be in government, I'm not suggesting that the Church should look to government to solve all its problems or answer its prayers. The governments of this world are not the kingdom of God. We live in the world but are not of this world, and yet we are commanded to go into the world.

> *They are not of the world, just as I am not of the world.*
>
> John 17:16 (ESV)
>
> *And he [Jesus] said to them, "Go into all the world and proclaim the gospel to the whole creation."*
>
> Mark 16:15 (ESV)

To fully understand the purpose of government, the Church needs wisdom from God and knowledge from His Word. Could it be that earthly government positions are a training ground for ruling and reigning with Christ for all eternity? Perhaps the stakes are higher than we suppose.

Instead of avoiding the political process, let's engage it. *"Go into all the world"* doesn't just mean standing behind a pulpit or taking your family to a third world nation. There are many ways to impart the gospel of Christ to humanity. Ministry is sacrifice—reaching out and giving of ourselves for Christ and His kingdom.

Christians must participate in government as if it were a ministerial calling. Governmental service is a place where God can use a person to orchestrate great change and fulfill His divine plan for His people. It is a place where history is made. It is an institution through which God can use the Church to change the world.

> I am concluding this book with a powerful and persuasive statement from Fr. Frank Pavone:
>
> The Church does not have a political mission, she nevertheless has a political responsibility to bear witness to those moral truths without which the common good—which is the very purpose for which governments are instituted—cannot survive. These moral truths are basic and go beyond the bounds of any denominational beliefs. Because they are truths, they must shape public policy. Not only do individuals have a duty to obey God, but so do governments. Moreover, the people of God do not lose their citizenship on earth by virtue of the fact that they are citizens of heaven (see Phil. 3:20). If anything, our belief in heaven makes us more concerned about the earth, not less concerned. Why? Because the good that we bring about on earth is not lost in the next world but remains and grows. Human life and activity continue in the world to come, which is why they are so important to us now. Christians have a duty to be politically active, to register and vote, to lobby and educate candidates and elected officials, and to speak up about the issues that

affect the common good. Now is the time, now is the challenge. No longer are we to think of our religion as a purely "private matter." Christ taught in public, and he was crucified in public. Now risen from the dead, he places us in the public arena, with the commission to make disciples of all nations (see Mt. 28:18-20). May we not fail him or our nation.[59]

About The Author

Mary Salamon resides in the Pacific Northwest. She was the publisher of Marysville Tulalip Life Magazine. She served as the Washington State Leader for the Governors Prayer Team.

Mary is currently the overseer of Marysville House of Prayer, a regional leader for the National Day of Prayer, and a writer for the Marysville Globe.

She is the mother of three sons and grandmother of five beautiful grandchildren. She is available for speaking engagements at local civic events, churches and conferences.

You can contact her at:

mary@thequeenbeeofabsolutelyeverything.com

marysalamon@facebook.

Notes

1. Robert Putnam, Bowling Alone, 42.

2. Sire, The Universe Next Door, 20.

3. Paine, Thomas Paine: Collected Writings, 13.

4. Boyd, God of the Possible, page 102.

5. Dictionary.com, s.v. "occupy."

6. Strong's Handi-Reference Concordance, s.v. "thrones," "dominion," and "power."

7. Robertson and Slosser, The Secret Kingdom, 199.

8. http://www.biblearchaeology.org/post/2010/02/23/Joseph-in-Egypt-Part-II.aspx.

9. http://www.biblearchaeology.org/post/2010/02/23/Joseph-in-Egypt-Part-II.aspx

10. http://www.biblearchaeology.org/post/2010/03/04/Joseph-in-Egypt-Part-III.aspx.

11. Ibid.

12. http://www.biblearchaeology.org/post/2010/04/05/Joseph-in-Egypt-Part-V.aspx.

13. Ibid.

14. Aling, Egypt and Bible History, 74.

15. Westbrook and Wells, Everyday Law, 22-23.

16. Ibid., 22-24.

17. https://en.wikipedia.org/wiki/Code_of_Hammurabi.

18. Cundall and Morris, Judges and Ruth, 136.

19. Ackerman, Warrior, Dancer, Seductress, Queen, 29 and 42-43.

20. Oxford English Dictionary, s.v. "just."

21. Dictionary.com, s.v. "covet."

22. Finkelstein and Silberman, The Bible Unearthed, 181-182.

23. Ibid.

24. Quoted in Lambert, Babylonian Wisdom Literature, 3-4.

25. Baldwin, Daniel, 92.

26. http://jbq.jewishbible.org/assets/Uploads/6/jbq_6_3_final.pdf, 115-117.

27. Boice, Nehemiah, 126-128.

28. http://ntwrightpage.com/Wright_Paul_Caesar_Romans.htm.

29. http://www.abarim-publications.com/Dictionary/m/m-l-ht. html#.W1gPasJ9jIU.

30. Weinfeld, Deuteronomy.

31. Patton and Patton Jr., War as I Knew It.

32. Ibid.

33. Saia, Why Pray?, 31, 36, 38, 41.

34. Prince, Praying for the Government, 229-236.

35. https://www.ifapray.org/resources/prayer-guides-and-resources/.

36. Catt and Shuler, Woman Suffrage and Politics.

37. https://tuesdayshorse.wordpress.com/2009/01/13/horses-have-a-hero-in-new-yorks-tedisco-us/.

38. https://dailygazette.com/article/2009/12/19/1220_buster.

39. https://www.thepetitionsite.com/petition/.

40. https://www.thepetitionsite.com/cause-to-successful-petition/.

41. From the notes of a Family Policy Institute workshop called Olympia 301.

42. http://www.goodhousekeeping.com/life/parenting/a39575/my-neighbor-saved-my-sons-life.

43. Bethune, "The End of Neighbors." https://www.macleans.ca/society/the-end-of-neighbours/.

44. https://www.blueletterbible.org//lang/lexicon/lexicon.

cfm?Strongs=G4139&t=NKJV.

45. http://www.denverdweller.com/neighborhood-community-reads/.

46. https://www.forbes.com/sites/steveforbes/2011/09/09/remembering-911-the-rudy-giuliani-interview/#1c18e0503a7d

47. https://www.commentarymagazine.com/culture-civilization/history/giuliani-leadership-on-911/.

48. https://wacities.org/docs/default-source/resources/mayorscouncilmembershandbookwebec4f3b49b78160ed9eadff0000bbe4eb.pdf?sfvrsn=0

49. https://work.chron.com/role-police-officer-8056.html.

50. https://firstliberty.org/.

51. https://firstliberty.org/cases/.

52. http://capta6.org/docs/whatdoesthePTAdo.pdf.

53. http://www.steelecanyonathleticboosters.com/uploads/1/3/3/3/13337542/schs_boosters_membership_generic.pdf.

54. http://www.colorincolorado.org/article/parent-participation-how-get-involved-your-childs-school-activities.

55. Aristotle, Politics.

56. https://www.opendoorsusa.org/christian-persecution/world-watch-list/about-the-ranking/ and https://www.opendoorsusa.org/christian-persecution/stories/5-gut-wrenching-facts-north-korean-prison-camps/.

57. https://diplomacy.state.gov/discoverdiplomacy/diplomacy101/people/170341.htm.

58. https://en.wikipedia.org/wiki/J._Christopher_Stevens

59. http://www.priestsforlife.org/library/4377-caesar-must-obey-god.

Bibliography

Ackerman, Susan. Warrior, Dancer, Seductress, Queen: Women in Judges and Biblical Israel. New York: Doubleday, 1998.

Aling, Charles F. Egypt and Bible History: From Earliest Times to 1000 B.C. Grand Rapids, Michigan: Baker, 1981.

Aristotle. Politics. Sage Publications, Inc., 2006.

Baldwin, Joyce G. Daniel. Downers Grove, Illinois: IVP Academic, 1978.

Boice, James Montgomery. Nehemiah. Grand Rapids, Michigan: Baker, 2005.

Boyd, Gregory A. God of the Possible: A Biblical Introduction to the Open View of God. Gale, Cengage Learning, 2000.

Catt, Carrie Chapman and Nettie Rogers Shuler. Woman Suffrage and Politics. 1923.

Cundall and Morris. Judges and Ruth. Downers Grove, Illinois: Tyndale, 1968.

Finkelstein, Israel, and Neil Asher Silberman. The Bible Unearthed: Archaeology's New Vision of 138 Ancient Israel and the Origin of Its Sacred Texts. New York: Touchstone, 2002.

Lambert, W.G. Babylonian Wisdom Literature. Oxford, 1960.

Patton, George S. and George S. Patton Jr. War as I Knew It. Boston: Houghton Mifflin Co., 1995.

Prince, Derek. Praying for the Government. Derek Prince Ministries, 2012. Kindle edition.

Putnam, Robert. Bowling Alone: The Collapse and Revival of American Community. New York: Simon and Shuster, 2000.

Paine, Thomas. Thomas Paine: Collected Writings. New York, New York: The Library of America, 1995.

Robertson, Pat, and Bob Slosser. The Secret Kingdom. Nashville,

Tennessee: W Publishing Group, 1992.

Saia, Michael. Why Pray? Edmonds, Washington, 2014.

Sire, James W. The Universe Next Door: A Basic Worldview Catalog. Intervarsity Press, 2009. E-book.

Weinfeld, Moshe, and S. Sperling. Deuteronomy. Gale, 2007. E-book.

Westbrook, Raymond, and Bruce Wells. Everyday Law in Biblical Israel: An Introduction. Louisville, Kentucky: Westminster John Knox, 2009.

Yamauchi, Edwin M. Persia and the Bible. Grand Rapids, Michigan: Baker, 1990.

57514996R00114

Made in the USA
Columbia, SC
10 May 2019